Self-confidence

Alankrita

Publishers
Pustak Mahal®, Delhi

J-3/16 , Daryaganj, New Delhi-110002
☎ 23276539, 23272783, 23272784 • *Fax:* 011-23260518
E-mail: info@pustakmahal.com • *Website:* www.pustakmahal.com

Sales Centres
10-B, Netaji Subhash Marg, Daryaganj, New Delhi-110002
☎ 23268292, 23268293, 23279900 • *Fax:* 011-23280567
E-mail: rapidexdelhi@indiatimes.com

Branch Offices
Bangalore: ☎ 22234059
E-mail: pmblr@sancharnet.in • pustak@sancharnet.in
Mumbai: ☎ 22010941
E-mail: rapidex@bom5.vsnl.net.in
Patna: ☎ 3094193 • *Telefax:* 0612-2302719
E-mail: rapidexptn@rediffmail.com
Hyderabad: *Telefax:* 040-24737290
E-mail: pustakmahalhyd@yahoo.co.in

This book was earlier printed under the title
"Nurture Self-confidence to achieve..."

© **Pustak Mahal, Delhi**

ISBN 81-223-0693-4

Edition : 2006

The Copyright of this book, as well as all matter contained herein (including illustrations) rests with the Publishers. No person shall copy the name of the book, its title design, matter and illustrations in any form and in any language, totally or partially or in any distorted form. Anybody doing so shall face legal action and will be responsible for damages.

Printed at : United Colour Offset Press, Delhi

Dedicated to My Father,
Late Shri A.N. Banerjee

Preface

Mother Earth is inhabited by approximately 6 billion people out of which more than one-sixth of the people are living in the Indian Sub-continent. Amidst this sea of humanity, there are only a handful of men and women who are able to achieve greatness. They start revolutions, create epochs, author the annals of history, discover new worlds and pioneer novel concepts. These men and women come to control the destinies of millions and give new dimensions to human existence. There are always some attributes that are responsible for making a life great. These may be either mental qualities or the qualities of heart, body or soul. This book is a humble attempt to identify the persons who possessed some of such qualities. If one reads it, it is certain that he/she will gather the self-confidence which is absolutely required to lead a good life.

GREATNESS is never the prodigy of circumstances, it is always the outcome of great thoughts and their strategic implementation with utmost confidence.

It must be clearly understood that "Great" in the apparent sense is not a synonym of "big". A Great man can nevertheless be humble in mortal gains but his deeds may carry within him, the intrinsic value of greatness.

This book contains innumerable stories, instances and lives that have left for us the imprints for future life. Whatever we possess today is owing to the sacrifices made by those handful of men, women and events which have transformed the very meaning of life.

Whatever may be our endowments, background, situation or time, we must try our level best to comprehend and nurture our true potential. Why not explore it?

In my previous book **Positive Self Transformation**, I gave exhaustive indications towards the true meaning of life as well as its positive transformation. In this book, I wish the reader to catch hold of the impulses that will enable him to find the right slot in the whirlwind towards Greatness by enhancing level of SELF-CONFIDENCE to unattained heights.

Here we commence a breathtaking journey towards greatness and exploring a world of Self-confidence.

❏❏

Contents

Preface   *v*

Chapter One

JOURNEY TOWARDS GREATNESS THROUGH SELF-CONFIDENCE

• The Benchmark of Greatness	9
• Breaking the Inertia	17
• Forming a Mini-Universe Within	20
• Inspirations	23
• Translating Ideas into Life	25

Chapter Two

THE GREATEST EVENTS IN HUMAN HISTORY

• Learning from Our Past	28
• The Birth of America	29
• The French Revolution	36
• Communism Takes on the World	39
• The Renaissance of Japan	40
• The Great Sons of Modern India	47

Chapter Three

CULTIVATING SELF-CONFIDENCE

• The Psychic Influence at Birth	52
• The Years of Adolescence	54
• Always a Winner!	60

Chapter Four

CHURNING OUT A GREAT PERSONALITY

• The Personality Traits of Great People	63
• The Magnetic Aura of Great Leaders	70
• The Art of Communication & Oratory	78
• Revealing the Genius within you	84
• Stealing the Hearts of Millions!	86

Chapter Five

STRATEGY FOR BUILDING CONFIDENCE

• Prioritizing	89
• Planning	92
• Time-scheduling	93
• The Significance of Motivation	94

Chapter Six

OVERCOMING HURDLES ON THE WAY TO GREATNESS

• The Possible Hurdles	96
• Winning Over Odd Circumstances	99
• The Foes of Greatness	104
• The Greatest Comebacks in Human History	108
• The Great Virtues	111

Chapter One
Journey towards Greatness through Self-confidence

The Benchmark of Greatness

> *If a man hasn't discovered something that he will die for, he isn't fit to live.*
> —Martin Luther-I

These words are as stirring and true as the life of its believer. In a few words, the very meaning of human existence has been summed up. Life is nothing more than a search - a continuous search for a cause to live and die to be governed by the thoughts and dreams and propelled by a concealed urge to achieve Greatness. In this vast sea of humanity, let us take a solemn pledge - a pledge to accomplish that for which we are born, to conquer our follies and failings and stand apart from the teeming millions, as the one who leaves his footprints for others to walk upon. But before we commence our journey towards greatness, we must contemplate upon its nature and try to find a coherence with it in our own short life.

Defining Greatness

Greatness can be termed as the measurement of the 'intrinsic value' of a person or his deeds. Greatness is never tainted with selfish motives. Rather, it is guided by a strong motive which is the 'welfare' of mankind. A man can earn lots of money, build palaces, provide the best to his family and wallow in the swamp of glory, but can't reach greatness if his efforts are guided only towards self elevation. On the other hand, a soldier fighting for his country after putting everything at stake or a modest social worker dedicating his life for social upliftment without caring for his personal well-being, can definitely be termed as Great. Greatness has within its bosom, the central theme of "Giving" - giving knowledge, cultivating faith, giving solace, giving peace and above all giving up yourself for the good of others.

It has been truly said by Khalel Gibran -

You give but little when you give of your possessions. It is when you give of yourself that you truly give.

The benchmark of GREATNESS comprises the following virtues:

Possessing a worthwhile cause

In the words of Swami Vivekananda "**Life is short, Give up to a great cause.**" It is only when a person rises above his own petty self and dedicates himself to a cause, that he sows the seeds of an enlightened life. He becomes an embodiment of an ideology and gradually loses his own tiny existence. This is the first benchmark towards greatness. He and his cause become one. The cause can be social, moral or patriotic.

One such man was Martin Luther. On October 31, 1517, when Martin Luther was nailing his thesis upon the door of the church at Wittenburg, criticizing the sale of indulgences, never did he realize that he was going to give birth to a new religious sect called the **Protestants.** Amidst turbulent opposition from the greatest powers in Europe, he kept his cause glowing like a radiant sun. What kept him moving was his unflinching faith in his cause which he believed was the voice of his conscience.

I can and will retract nothing, as it is dangerous to act against one's conscience was his confident proclamation. Martin Luther was quick to recognize the spiritual fervour within him. He was grossly unsatisfied with religious abuses doled out by the priests. His strong religious convictions grew into a rage and he threw his entire life to the Reformation of Christianity. His contributions to religion helped to transform the medieval world into the modern.

- *Driven by a single obsession*

    Great men and women always live with "one mission". Their minds are filled by an obsession to accomplish their mission. They are never daunted by circumstances or conditions, rather their eyes are fixed upon what they desire to achieve. Day and night, their thoughts revolve around their mission.

In ancient India, a little before the battle **Mahabharata** was fought, sage *Dronacharya* was assigned the task of teaching archery to his disciples—young princes of *Hastinapur* among whom the name of *Arjuna* stands apart. As a young boy, he had only one obsession - to be the world's greatest archer. One fine afternoon, all the princes were asked to aim at the eye of a clay bird. To test their concentration, Dronacharya enquired all the princes "What do you all see?" Some princes pointed towards the trees, the surroundings, some towards the well and the river. It was only Arjun who said "I only see the bird's eye." The surroundings made no effect on him, for he had just one thing in his mind - his goal of becoming the greatest archer of the world.

Our Ancient history stands as a testimony to the fact that our country has produced so many great archers but none can match the stature of Arjun.

Unchanging conviction

Swami Vivekananda puts it very aptly "**I will drink the ocean, to preserve soul. Mountains will crumble into dust at my feet**". Such men of great mettle erect a fortress of strong and unmoving conviction around themselves which none can pierce. They always live with the feeling that they are born to accomplish some great task. For them, it is the cause that matters and not the condition.

One such hero was David Livingstone - the man who accorded respect and knowledge to the Dark Continent of Africa. Amidst the negative pursuits of his father, the dangerous journeys across Africa, the physical dual with a lion in which he almost lost his left arm and the ailing health of his children, he crossed the insurmountable Kalahari Desert and discovered numerous unknown rivers like the Zouga, Zambezi, and lands like Landa in Central Africa. He was nearly crippled with fever, ill-health, lack of food and equipment but he continued his adventures until he became a hero. Eventually he died in the lap of the mysterious continent of Africa.

Nothing could daunt him.... not even death for he continued to live in the hearts of millions of adventure lovers around the world. Africa definitely owes a never-ending debt to him.

- **Consistent labour**

    And thou wilt give thyself relief, if thou doest every act of thy life, as if it were the last

    –Marcus Aurelius

We must work in such a way towards our mission as if every moment is the last moment of our life. Great people reap the fruits of their incessant labour. Their only concern is towards the work which they undertake without thinking of its results. They are always guided by the 'spirit of action' and not by the jugglery of words. Hence the most appropriate way to achieve greatness is to "burn the midnight lamp" both literally as well as figuratively and continue working towards the attainment of the cause.

Therefore one of the **Upanishads,** the sacred Hindu texts, echoes with these powerful words:

Arise, Awake and stop not till the goal is reached.

When passivity takes to labour - actions take place. Peter the Great of Russia was a raw and uncivilized ruler of a mighty empire. He set out to study, acquire knowledge and make himself appropriate for his empire. "Myself a pupil, I seek teachers", was a seal that he carried with himself.

He acquired immense knowledge and returned to his native place Russia for initiating the process of westernization and reforms. Russia at that time had no navy and seaports. Peter was determined to establish both.

In 1695, Peter made his first attack upon Azov but was utterly defeated. But he was committed to his plans. He made another attempt. This time he met with convincing success. With this success, he poured in large sums of money to maintain a fleet of ships in the waters that he had conquered.

Two years later, he sent a large number of Russians to Holland, England, Italy and Germany to acquire knowledge about civilizations. He himself studied Architecture, Mechanics, Fortification, Printing, Anatomy and Astronomy in Holland. His labour continued.

From Holland, he went to England where he learnt the theory and practice of ship-building. Apart from this, he gave his mind to many new things such as setting up universities, hospitals, Royal societies, cathedrals and churches in his country for which he visited all these in England.

Not only this, Peter also toiled in shipyards as an apprentice to learn about naval establishments and dockyards.

Although Peter had many vices, his energy was boundless. He undertook the biggest and the smallest tasks with the equal amount of ease. All his drawbacks could somehow be compensated with his extreme hardwork.

He exhausted himself in the endeavour to build up his country. He took up the responsibility of transforming a semi-Asiatic state into one of the most developed regions of Europe. His efforts bore fruit because of his consistent labour.

Devoid of evil inclines

All great men have one thing in common - their love for humanity and their hatred for evil. Before venturing out for a mission "clean up your soul" and submit yourself to a life of goodness. If you fail to conquer evil, you will certainly fail to enter the kingdom of the great. Every great movement which has flourished on the earth, has been triggered off by the "essence of nobility". The renowned dictum "From log cabin to Whitehouse" sums up the entire life of Abraham Lincoln. A poor nomad born in a log cabin, lost his mother at an early age, hit hard by the humiliations of slavery and facing tough attacks from the US press, Abraham Lincoln went on to become one of the greatest men, US has ever produced - conquering the hearts of millions of people with his sense of justice and sincerity. His ascent to the post of the President of USA was not of as much significance as his notable contributions in the field of social justice and the abolition of slavery and amendment of the Constitution of America. His life echoed with one principle - the benefit of mankind.

"I have done nothing to make any Human being remember that I have lived. Yet what I wish to live for is to connect my name with the events of my day

and generation, to link my name with something which will be of interest to my fellow-men," said Abraham Lincoln

This was written when he was a young man of thirty-two. He had more misery in life than happiness. Once while he was trying to come out of a fit of depression, he strongly felt like committing suicide. This man could not have asked for more as from a poor man, born in a log cabin, he rose to become the President of the United States of America. His life is almost an epic of U.S.A which almost owes him today, its existence as a Nation.

Born on 12th February, 1809 in Kentucky, Abraham was the son of a wandering carpenter. He was fascinated by the greenery and far away lands. At the age of four, Abraham began his wanderings along with his family. His father, being extremely restless moved to Indiana. For one year, the family had to live in floorless, half-built camp made up of uncut logs. Life was extremely difficult as the region was swampy. Animals did not thrive and human beings began falling victims to Malaria. While facing hardships, Abraham lost his mother on account of a fatal disease. After the death of his mother, family began to wander to distant lands. It was then that Abraham, for the first time saw his step mother. A new life began for Abraham. His new mother insisted that he should go to school. Abraham, known as Abe, began his educational career in fits and starts. He learnt some reading and writing. But from that day onwards he began to read everything that came on his way. He grew up into a strong man but was known for his eccentricity for he talked on various topics and tried to imitate preachers and orators.

The turning point in his life came in 1828 when for the first time he was exposed to the outside world infested with slavery. He began his career by carrying agricultural produce to New Orleans by boat. It gave him the opportunity to study the condition of Negro slaves. He was moved to see their appalling condition.

Abraham Lincoln found the mission of his life. He decided to abolish slavery from America. His journey towards Greatness commenced when he chose a mission that would alleviate the condition of the Blacks.

Later on, Abraham Lincoln became the manager of the store where he used to sell his agricultural products. There he engaged himself in extensive reading as well as in local politics by acting as a clerk of the local polls.

Being the scholar of the district, he became a participator in local political debates and was drawn in towards politics. But due to his interest in politics, he almost became insolvent in his store business. But he continued his involvement with politics.

Abraham Lincoln became the candidate for the Legislature in the year 1834. But another pursuit caught his interest during those days. It was law. Abraham formed a law partnership firm with William H. Herndon who later became his biographer.

An address that he gave in New York gave him a nationwide reputation. People were surprised to see that an uncouth, ill-clad, lanky lawyer had the power to sway the masses. The press began to attack him severely. He was termed as a "third-rate country lawyer, with poor grammar, clumsy jokes, gorilla like looks and a shabby dressing sense". The slave owning aristocrats despised him. But he became popular among the masses for whom he was fighting.

Abraham Lincoln met with one misfortune after another. One of the gravest among them was the bad relations with his wife and the illness of both his sons. But amidst all these problems, Abraham Lincoln never hesitated from signing a proclamation for the complete emancipation of the slaves.

Finally after umpteen trials and tribulations, Abraham Lincoln succeeded in accomplishing the mission of his life - the thirteenth amendment bill was passed and the Constitution of the United States of America was amended. Slavery was abolished from USA.

Finally, on April 14, 1865, Abraham Lincoln assumed the highest post in the land. He was elected as the President of the country.

His sense of Equality, deep-rooted benevolence, forgiveness and faith in Justice ensured his sublime greatness.

He possessed a great sagacity to guiding people through the tumults of mighty revolutions with the help of deep religiosity, an admirable singleness of purpose, a flaming passion to free his country from the bonds of slavery. It was a luminous example of utmost honesty and purity, the possession of keen and inexplicable magnetism and the moderation in temperament that made him soothing to his subordinates.

Abraham Lincoln was the architect of his own destiny. He rose with every opportunity, conquered every crisis, performed every duty. Civilization will hold his name in eternal renown as a patriot, leader and liberator. He truly possessed Supreme confidence which provided him best opportunities in life.

Breaking the Inertia

Building "Self-confidence" is not a day's work. It needs years and years of dedication, perseverance and patience. But good work can only be done if the thoughts are moulded accordingly. To mould our thoughts into a perfect cast, it is necessary for us to let loose our imagination till they crystallize into a specific pattern.

Now, what is inertia and how can we break it?

Inertia, in this context, is nothing but the inability to break loose.

Since our very childhood, *we are afraid to dream, to imagine and to allow our thoughts to break free*. The reasons for this can be many. Let us discuss some of them:

The first and foremost cause of inertia is *Insecurity*.

Insecurity

Every person possesses an insecurity regarding his sustenance. How will I maintain my livelihood? How will I meet my family's expenses? are the common concerns of one and all although these concerns are quite genuine. A person must learn the art of making his survival interests, a part of his mission and not vice-versa. Try to take out a middle path between your family responsibilities and your mission.

Trample Upon Insecurity

All great people have had difficulties in fulfilling their family needs, but they never undermined their zeal. Karl Marx (whom we shall discuss later) was confronted by extreme penury. He found it difficult to meet his both ends. His family reeled under poverty. But he gave to the world one of the greatest movements for the betterment of the poor and downtrodden.

Sacrifice yourself for the family, the family for the neighbourhood, the neighbourhood for the city, the city for the state, the state for the country and the country for Humanity. For there is no duty on this earth which comes above Humanity.

- *Family pressure*

    The second major cause of our mental inertia is family pressure. It might be possible that one wants to become a great musician but his parents want him to become a doctor. In this case, what will he like to do?

- *Never succumb to pressure*

    If one strongly believes that he possesses the aptitude of becoming a great musician, then he must not succumb to pressure. One should stick to one's aim and be truthful to it. One must have faith in one's convictions and then proceed. On the other hand, if he succumbs to pressure against his own will, he will neither be able to do justice to his profession nor to his parents. He will remain half-hearted towards his profession and unhappy with his parents. One must be confident about what he desires to achieve in life.

Lack of Confidence

Lack of confidence is also a significant reason for allowing our thinking to break loose. If one feels that he is having the potential of becoming a TV Artist and wants to render information, knowledge and entertainment to people across the country, the only thing which would impede him would be lack of confidence.

- *Nurture the confidence*

    Confidence is like a plant - it needs to be manured, watered and exposed before sunlight. It needs the manure of a mission, the water of continuous self-persuasion and exposed to the sunlight of skills and hardwork.

    We have to work hard with our thoughts as well as our confidence and at no moment in our life, allow it to perish. The quality of the plant depends upon the quality of the soil, similarly the quality of our work will directly depend upon the quality of our thoughts. So fill your mind with the greatest thoughts and out of that will emerge great work.

    Once you overcome the impediments that come in way of our thoughts, you must unleash the forces of your mind. Release your creative imagination and aim for the highest. The amount of efforts that are needed for survival are no less than the amount of endeavours required to become great. Then why settle for something less. Greatness is just a matter of attitude, perceptions and implementation. Give vent to your thoughts—aim for the highest.

Napoleon once said, "Forty centuries are looking down upon you. So March on! It is the spirit which works and not the hands. Break yourself free from the crippling influence of "inertia".

It is never a sin to dream.

Never hesitate to dream. Always keep them sublime and keep in mind that you have to follow your dreams till their fulfilment. Let not your thoughts become a victim of inertia.

Going Against Usual Norms

No great work has ever been accomplished without opposition. If going against systems is a sin then every great social and spiritual leader is a sinner. If you have to break certain norms for the betterment of mankind and for the fulfilment of your noble mission, go ahead—the Divine grace will bestow His choicest blessings upon you.

If you are still contemplating, your doubts will be certainly put to rest, once you fortify your thoughts - let's see how.

Forming a Mini-Universe Within

Once you have broken your "inertia" and "dared to dream" about your mission, you have already commenced your journey towards greatness. Now the next thing which you are required to do is to "fortify" your thoughts. To make sure that whatever dream you are nurturing within remains with you till its final accomplishment. How can you do that?

Our mind is divided into three portions - the conscious, the sub-conscious and the super-conscious. The last i.e. super-conscious is only active in men who attain divinity. So, we are only concerned with the first two. Fill your conscious mind with thoughts about your mission by perpetual contemplation. What is perpetual contemplation? It involves:

Self Persuasion

Persuade yourself constantly by reading motivational literature, gaining knowledge about the ways and means of achieving your mission and also by nurturing your thoughts in the same direction.

- *Fixing your ideal*

    You should begin with fixing up such a person as your ideal who has already reached the zenith of the field you intend to pursue. Try to study his life in detail. Search for the qualities he or she possessed. Try to learn from the mistakes which he committed. It will help you frame-up your own future image and enhance your confidence level.

- *Perpetual contemplation on your aim*

    After waking up in the morning, repeat your aim several times. Abstain from loose thinking that can distract you from your path.

- *Let each day be another step*

    Our entire life is a ladder and each day is a step towards the top of the ladder. Hence do not waste a single moment. At the end of each day, you should feel that you have taken another step towards your mission.

    You can try out a game. Keep 365 coins with you in reserve. Let each coin represent a day. If you feel that you haven't fully utilized the day, take one coin out from the reserve fund and put it away. In case you feel that you have outdone your day's target- add 25 cents to the fund. At the end of every week, month and year, calculate your reserves. You will be able to measure the worth of time in tangible terms.

Try to form a Universe within you, which remains fortified. In order to create this Mini Universe as well as to fortify it, you need a very strong defence mechanism. Defend the boundaries of your Universe with a strong General - your "conscience". Your conscience must keep a check on every outside element (thought) that enters your Universe as well as departs from it. The only thing that should be borne in mind is never to disturb the harmonious balance that pertains in your mini-universe.

If this mini-universe is your mind, then there are surely distractors or impediments, who are waiting to destroy your equilibrium. Let us see which are those distractors that can harm your Universe.

Conditions

Conditions in life will keep varying from time to time. Try to remain balanced under every condition. For that, you must have strong faith in your mission. Secondly, you must pray regularly because prayer helps you to develop faith and enhance your internal strength. Prayer will help you to protect your mini-universe from all vagaries of the external world.

- *Discouragement*

    If you get daunted because of discouragement, it proves that somehow or the other you are still lacking faith in your own mission. The person who believes in himself, nothing can affect him adversely.

- *Depression*

    Another problem which you may face very often is that of depression. While pursuing the aims, one may be confronted with innumerable problems. The problems can be multifarious - of health, of money, of social acceptance or of family uncertainties. These difficulties are a part of any great mission. It is like a plant of rose whose beauty gets accentuated by the presence of thorns. No great work has ever been achieved without hurdles. Hence, whatever problems come your way they must be dealt sportingly without letting the devil of depression win. Depression not only reduces the level of motivation, it also saps out vital energy from your mind and body. Let us consider now how to tackle the problem of depression.

- *Tackle the problem of depression*

    - Always try to strike the problem at the root.
    - Try to take your mind away from the depressing factor and focus it on different activities.
    - Take some time off from ponderous work schedules and relax.
    - Practise some mild breathing exercises, like slow inhalation and exhalation.
    - Repeat regularly to yourself, "Nobody can shatter my confidence."

    Always protect your mini-universe against all odds, because within that tiny world rests your entire future.......Let us consider now the value of inspiration in building Self-confidence.

Inspirations

The dream that man weaves is always woven with the help of inspirations. These inspirations can either be derived from great events or great experiences, but these dreams certainly become the yardstick of a man's character. We all possess an uncanny knack of learning from inspiring factors and events. But we must not overlook small incidents or even insignificant beings who are inspiring us every moment.

Let us begin with the 5 elements of Nature that have been the continuous source of inspiration for mankind since eternity. We are all made up of these five elements and we are ultimately going to blend into all of them. So why not derive certain inspirations from them!

Air

Air is the source of survival of every living animal on the earth. It keeps an equal eye upon the rich and the poor, the famous and the notorious or the high class and the low class. Its message for humanity is that of "Equanimity".

Fire

Fire can give life as well as take life. It depends upon how we use it. It is neither a friend nor a foe. Rather it is a thing to be used prudently. If utilized properly, it can give us food and energy and if handled carelessly, it can cause us injury and devastation.

Water

Water possesses the unique attribute of perpetuity. Whatever the conditions might be, water can never remain still. It keeps moving from one place to another. Its velocity depends upon various factors but its movement is never affected. It can never be broken, cut or destroyed. Its flexibility makes it ever existent.

Earth

Since millions of years, man has trampled upon earth yet she has been silently bearing every deed of man. She possesses the extremes of endurance and patience for the fulfilment of her mission - helping mankind to survive.

People who are desirous of achieving their mission in life must imbibe endurance and patience like mother earth. In that case, she is the greatest source of man's inspiration.

Sky (Ether)

Why is the sky so significant? It is important because it gives mankind the idea of vastness. It is the crown of the Lord which never comes to an end.

Another synonym of life is 'expansion'. In the words of Swami Vivekananda, **"Expansion is life, contraction is death"**. Never restrict your thinking, let it grow till it encompasses the entire humanity. "Keep growing till you are able to provide shelter to all those who are beneath you." This is one of the keys for unlocking the treasure of 'greatness' and self-confidence.

Translating Ideas into Life

It is true that if a new idea clicks, it can turn an ordinary man into a genius. The man who discovered the idea of gravity was none other than the great Newton who churned out a brilliant idea from a small incidence like the falling of an apple. His main achievement was to discover the concept of 'gravity', which we made it known to the entire humankind. This simple thought which struck his mind required years of tenacious research. When it got converted into life, it made an ordinary farm boy, one of the greatest scientists the world has ever produced. If he did not possess the capability of converting dreams into ideas, he would have remained anonymous and insignificant throughout his life like millions of other farmers of his age and time.

Ideas lose their significance till they are translated into life. Every single idea needs to be planted, first in the mind and then on the ground.

Now the question arises - how to translate ideas into life?

Let us take it step by step.

Step One

Prepare a Plan

Before you begin to translate ideas into life, you must possess a clear conception of what you actually desire to do. For that, you must have a clear-cut plan before yourself. The plan must be tangible, quantified and scheduled. Without a proper plan your journey towards greatness will become as aimless as a rudderless ship which is oblivious of its destination.

Step Two

Make a Schedule

Once the plan is ready, you should then discreetly divide it into 3 phases. The present, the immediate future and the future.

Whatever is mentioned in the immediate future, it must be taken up in the right earnest. It must be implemented in your day to day life.

Just one thing must be clearly underlined in your mind. Never take up any profession, just for the sake of maintaining your livelihood - if it is not in concomitance to your ultimate mission. It will not only sap out your precious time and energy, but will also lead to your deviation from the final goal.

Step Three

Revise your Plan

For the success in any task, it is necessary to revise the plan on time. So at the end of every week, try to analyze your progress towards your ultimate mission. See if you have moved even an inch towards your destination. You may also review your strategies from a time to time basis. However, every task should be time-bound so that you are compelled to fulfil your targets. The fulfilment of small commitments will give you the taste of success. This itself will be a major motivator for you in your journey towards success.

Step Four

Association with like minded people

In our journey towards greatness, we must be very careful regarding the kind of people we meet. You should avoid the company of those who are not supportive to your mission. You should also avoid friction with others because that spoils your mental peace and eventually leads to failure.

Besides following the above steps, a few other things are also necessary to follow. Among them are: Independence of thought and action. Human beings as well as animals cherish independence. Persons who are dependant on others for success may face 'dejection' - if that person does not accomplish the task given to him, 'dissatisfaction'- if he falls short of expectations and 'deceit' - if he is betrayed by the other on account of greed, jealousy or vindication. Hence independence of thought and action is necessary in order to insure man from all the three D's.

After winning over the three D's, you are ready to march towards greatness. But before marching forward, it is absolutely necessary to take a quick dip into the past. To know about the cherished deeds of great men and women, to analyze the mistakes that man had committed and also to choose the precious gems of wisdom from the greatest events in human history.

❏❏

Chapter Two

The Greatest Events in Human History

Learning from Our Past

The destiny of mankind has been shaped by innumerable great epochs. These events have been the milestones in the advancement of human civilization and have resulted in man's culmination to ultimate power, fame and glory. They within short periods, helped people to achieve that amount of greatness which even centuries of normal life would have failed to confer upon them. These events were a distinct display of human emotions ranging from extreme wrath to profound compassion, but they always revolved around one key motivating factor - man's perpetual desire to achieve the best.

In our journey towards greatness and nurturing confidence, we shall capture some of the finest and most significant moments of the past that have led to the conception and development of the modern world. I am confident that these breathtaking events will motivate us to carve out and work upon dreams that can become instrumental in sculpturing an even better future. Moreover, they will also provide an insight into the follies that our predecessors have committed and which we must avoid at all costs for the betterment of humankind.

All great events in World History have swung between two extremities of 'War' and 'Peace'. The nature of warfare

has been varying from time to time. It has been either military or political, philosophical or economic depending upon conditions. The attributes that have till now undermined the greatness of individuals or nations have been:
- Presence of ego, jealousy and greed
- Exploitation of the weak
- Misinterpretation of religious ideas
- Exaggeration of personal ambitions

The world has produced titans of great stature but they have ultimately fallen like ninepins before human justice.

Whatever dreams we cherish must be devoid of the above anomalies and caressed with a sense of **divine sublimity.**

Our History teaches us to nurture the attributes of :
- Self-Respect in place of Ego
- Freedom in place of Chaos
- Love in place of Lechery
- Ambition in place of Greed
- Complementation in place of Condemnation
- Utilization in place of Exploitation
- Harmony in place of Discord
- Rationality in place of Ritual
- Equilibrium in place of Emotion
- Spirituality in place of narrow Religion

As we take a plunge into our historical treasure, at many places we shall find the above attributes wanting and scarce. However, there were some people who kept the torch of greatness burning.

We shall begin our journey with the birth of a unique Nation - AMERICA.......

The Birth of America

America, today stands as the apparent leader among the

community of developed nations owing to its military, political and economic prowess. Although it existed as an entity since 15th Century, its birth as a nation took place after the American Revolution in 1776. Its journey towards material and military greatness commenced some 225 years ago when it was struggling to oust the Britishers from its own territory.

After the Seven Years War (1756-1763) fought between France and England, in which the French lost to the British, Britain won control over all the settlements in Northern America. From then onwards began the **Slave Trade** in Northern America. Hoards of people from the poor countries of Africa were forcibly imported and made to sweat out in huge tobacco plantations in the southern states of USA. The original inhabitants of the country - the *Red Indians* were a wandering race and never mingled with the local population.

The picture of America on the eve of the revolution could be painted on the canvas of our minds. The Northern States were under the dominion of somewhat educated people influenced by puritan traditions. The slaves were not employed, hence a sense of equality somewhat prevailed. The Southern States, with huge expanse of tobacco plantations were occupied by the Negro and the labour class, deeply frustrated because of injustice and exploitation. The natives of the country - the Red Indians were pushed to the Western parts of the country. All the colonists, although isolated from each other, began to blend with each other under the British influence which resulted in a cultural synthesis.

Trouble began in 1773, when the British government sought to compel the people to purchase tea from East India Company. The people revolted against this imposition and began to empty the ships loaded with tea by throwing the entire material overboard.

Later on in 1775, war began between England and her subjugated colonies. It began with the demand for a dominion government. Both the armies fought bravely for gaining supremacy over each other, but the fighting bore no fruit for the Americans.

Among the mass of umpteen people rose a dynamic, patriotic and courageous young man - His name was George Washington - who later became the First President of the United States of America.

Let us peep into the life of this humble farmer who rose to the greatest position in the history of USA.

George Washington

A young boy of eleven, having lost his father, went out to live with his step brother Lawrence. With diligence and sharpness he carved out a respectable place for himself in the field of farming. His enthusiasm always led him to experiment with novel ideas and equipment. He began to aim at bringing about notable reforms to American Animal Husbandry. He was looking forward to build up an Agricultural Empire in North America and to transform the face of agriculture in America. As he toiled day and night in his fields, his diligence bore fruit. Gradually, he became the proud owner of eight thousand acres of land with almost half of it under cultivation. In spite of gaining riches he kept account of ever single penny spent. He firmly believed in the proverb, "A penny saved is a penny earned."

The turning point of his life came in 1752, when Washington was appointed as an Adjutant in one of the military districts in Virginia. He was assigned the task to order the French to leave the disputed territory on the banks of the Ohio River. In 1754, with a small regiment of six hundred men, Washington marched into the disputed territory. Washington, with his intelligence and courage surprised the enemy and eventually vanquished them. This was the commencement of a series of battles fought bravely by Washington. In 1775, after the defeat and death of another French general, he was made the colonel and commander of all the combined Virginian forces.

He was never moved by grim experiences rather he was always ready to move into the face of dangers. On account of tough battles and falling health, Washington decided to return to his old occupation. But even after staying in it for quite a long period, his heart kept revolting against the vagaries of the British Rule. Washington was confronted with one blow after the other. First came the *Quebec Act*, which excluded settlers from the territory between Ohio and Mississippi. Being a landowner himself, he was deeply stung with this resolution. This Act was followed by the *Stamp Act* and the *Tea Act*, which completely bruised his pride.

Washington was ignited with the spirit of 'revolution' and 'freedom'.

Finally he firmed up the mission of his life, which was to achieve complete independence for all the states and bring them together into one nation, the American Nation.

It was the time when Washington was supported by a weak army. Besides, he was greatly perturbed because of the jealousy and incompetence of the Congress. His army was erratic, unpaid, ill-armed and half-fed. But in spite of every odds, in spite of bad weather and a number of defeats, Washington remained firm with his mission. He finally won the War of Independence.

Washington transferred his headquarters from Boston to New York. He was faced by a well-nurtured, well-armed and well-trained troop of 24,000 men having the intention of capturing New York. By mid-summer, the American forces had to quit Canada and the Northern frontier was completely exposed to British attack.

The most trying time came when Washington, badly beaten by the British army in Brandywine, was left to face cold and hunger. But he did not relent and did everything possible to keep his army together.

His unyielding perseverance met with fruits and matters started turning in his favour. He received a lot of support from the French Army. Two years later, in 1781. General Cornwallis who was representing the British Army in America surrendered and within a couple of years, America started establishing its independence.

Thus, under the sound leadership of George Washington, America started growing.

Later, in 1787, Washington was unanimously elected the First President of the federal Government. The constitution of the United States of America came into being.

Washington became the President championing the cause of a strong conservative government. He was not a votary of "unbridled freedom". Hence he did not support democracy at the outset. He firmly believed that people who are left to themselves become unfit to run their own government. George Washington did everything which he could do to combine the capitalists as well as the democrats.

The most glaring virtues that George Washington possessed and which made him great were his administration and statesmanship. Besides, he possessed courage and confidence and nothing on earth daunted him from his mission.

He possessed a serene composition and maintained tranquillity even under the most adverse circumstances with no trace of urgency or nervousness whatsoever.

Even on rare occasions and during strong provocations, he was able to subdue his anger. He possessed great self control. Besides, he had plenty of integrity. Never in his life did he try to achieve anything by dubious means.

"Modern History has not a more spotless character to commemorate. Invincible in resolution, firm in conduct, incorruptible in integrity, he brought to the helm of a victorious republic, the simplicity and innocence of rural life; he was forced into greatness by circumstances…….. and prevailed over his enemies rather by the wisdom of his designs and the perseverance of his character than by the extraordinary genius for the art of war. He was modest, without diffidence; sensible to the voice of fame, without vanity; independent and dignified, without either asperity or pride. He was a friend to liberty, but not to licentiousness- not to the dreams of the enthusiasts, but to those practical ideas inherited from her British descent."

The birth of America distinctly proves that a burning zeal of patriotism, an indomitable courage to fight injustice and establish Truth as well as a feeling of sacrifice for a great mission can lead to great events, even stimulated by half nourished, uncivilized and illiterate people.

The only ingredient required is a great mission coupled with an Iron will to accomplish it.

The Great Revolution that took place in 1776 in America surely established the foundations of a Democratic World. The declaration of independence framed during the same year unequivocally stated that "all men are born equal". It tried to remove the imprints of Racism although it did not succeed fully.

In order to carry on the task for generations, the people have to maintain the same amount of sublimity as kept by the Fathers of the Movements. Today we see that though that spirit of nationalism is still alive among the citizens of America, the younger generation is falling into the trap of drugs, violence and sex. If the greatness of spirit has to be maintained, Self control must be practised by every citizen of the country and this holds good for every person in the world.

In our individual journeys towards success, we shall come across men and women of all hues and shades. Some might possess an opulent social stature while others might be just crawling across a life of abject penury. Some people may succeed in impressing us while others may just fall far below our expectations. Amidst all such contradictions, we must always try to remain away from all personal prides and prejudices and undertake only those actions which are implied for the betterment of mankind. In our way towards greatness "none is our enemy". We must be careful about keeping our mission free from all vices and prejudices so that it remains untarnished.

All we require is to muster our inner strengths and get into action!

History has been a great motivating factor for all major events that have occurred in the world. The American Revolution resulting in the Birth of a united America and its break away from England, sparked off the flames of revolution and rebellion in the minds of the French. These flames invoked by ***Rousseau's*** writings assumed mammoth proportions.

Jean Jacques Rousseau - (1712-1778)

The pen is mightier than the sword is a saying which can beautifully explain the contribution of ***Rousseau*** in the ***French Revolution***. His pen accomplished within years what swords cannot accomplish in ages. He was a bizarre dreamer leading the way to independence for an enslaved nation.

Rousseau was born in Geneva (Switzerland) on June 28, 1712 in the family of a watchmaker who could hardly make his both ends meet. His mother expired within a fortnight of his birth. He began to read and enjoy novels and classics at a very early age under the guidance of his father. In 1722, he got caught in a conflict and was compelled to choose between banishment and imprisonment. He chose the former and escaped to Lyon. Rousseau during his adolescence underwent a lot of emotional turbulence. These were because of his fight against childhood passions, maintaining a decent livelihood, removing doubts about religion and God, learning the mannerisms of a civilized society and his struggle against illness. Till 1741, Rousseau kept hopping from one task to another and underwent through a 'futile' period in his life. During the late 40's in the 18th century he began to indulge in serious writing.

Rousseau realized that the monarchy of his times prevailing in France inflicted the greatest misery on the common masses. He lambasted the monarchy and aroused the youth with the fire of revolution. His **Social Contract** has been described as a fiery version of **Locke's Treatise** on Government.

We can safely conclude that it was only due to Rousseau's contribution that France rose from the vicious decay which had captured her entire social and political system and advanced towards one of the greatest events in world history - THE FRENCH REVOLUTION.

The French Revolution

The *French Revolution* took birth in the fields of poor peasants, inside the dingy rooms of crammed up houses and amidst the clamouring noise in busy market-places. It was fought with the sword of hunger, supported with the weapon of tears and nourished with the lances of empty bellies and stark realities.

This Great revolution is nothing but a saga of *the strong exploiting the weak* and eventually *the weak seizing their rights by the force of will*.

From 1789 to 1794, France saw the famished masses in action. The peasantry and the general masses found no representation in the Assembly. They were deprived of 'land to till' and were subjected to a life of extreme misery. They wanted to overthrow Monarchy headed by *King Louis VI* and his cruel wife *Queen Marie Antoinette.*

Although the **Rights of Man** were declared by some Nobles in the Assembly, it did little to ensure the Rights of common citizens. On January 21, 1793, the masses in Paris could bear no more. They stormed the palace of the King and dragged him out of the mansion along with his wife. Before a colossal crowd, the Royal couple were mercilessly beheaded in the "guillotine" by an enraged mob. This was the end of feudalism and serfdom and the commencement of *"Equality, Fraternity and Liberty".*

French Revolution was thus a "Fight for Truth" which met with a well deserved success. The agony of teeming millions fired into fervent patriotism, hammered such a revolution that thrived upon the shoulders of poverty-stricken masses.

Although *French Revolution* was almost over, the spirit of 'conquest' and 'transformation' was still looming large on the horizon. Out of this spirit rose the "Lion of France" –*Napoleon Bonaparte.*

Napoleon Bonaparte - The Lion of France

Perhaps, no man secured the imagination of his own and future times as did Nopolean Bonaparte. The little corporal who by his force of personality, comprehensible thinking, military genius and domineering ambition made himself emperor of France. He challenged the united forces of Europe.

Soldiers you are ill-fed and almost naked. The government owes you much but can do nothing for you. Your patience, your courage do you honour, but bring you neither advantage nor glory. I am about to lead you to the most fruitful plains of the world. Rich provinces, great cities will be in your power. There you will find honour and wealth and fame. With these words lectured to a frayed and famished

French army of which he had just taken command, Napoleon Bonaparte, the son of a frivolous Corsican Lawyer, had raised the curtain of a drama that held mankind enthralled for over a century.

Born in 1769 in the capital of Corsica, he received military training as a simple pensioner. By 1792, he became the captain of the artillery. His brilliance in war and his invincible courage made him win quick promotions. Within three years, he rose to the rank of General. And so there was Napoleon, young, courageous, ambitious, passionately in love and leading the French Army, which had almost achieved nothing. From capricious lover who was obsessed with his new bride, he turned into a man of blazing action.

His ambition can be well understood in his own words. He said, **The states of Europe must be melted into one Nation and Paris must be its capital.** In 1796 General Bonaparte launched his first campaign against the Austrians when he was just 27. Later in 1800, crossing the Alps with an army of about fifty thousand men he struck an inflicting defeat upon the Austrians who were making progress into Italy. The French uprooted the Austrian army and Napoleon became a conquering hero.

Greater than that was his reformation of the French administrative system. **Code Napoleon,** which he introduced was almost like a holy book for good governance. It was like a social gospel meant to codify French law. Not only that, he also initiated municipal and national developments for the betterment for the people of France. One of his main concerns was the upliftment of the standard of education and planned far reaching reforms in that area.

In 1804, barely at the age of 35, he became the undisputed Emperor of France. Then began his series of conquests. Prussia (Germany) went to war with Napoleon and paid a heavy cost. It was reduced to the position of a conquered state.

Regarding the concept of waging a war, Napoleon said:

At the beginning of a campaign thought should be expended whether an advance should be made or not, but when once the offensive has been assumed it should be maintained to the last extremity.

He never believed in looking back, after taking any major decision.

In three years, he ruled so well that it was more than the rule of kings for a Century.

The reasons for his greatness were:

Magnetic Personality
Ability to motivate people
Tremendous Courage
Strong Administrative power &
Extreme Self-Confidence

After going through two Great revolutions, we can understand how the people were suppressed by tyranny and power. There was a cry for equality all around. That cry began to spread in economic spheres too, giving birth to another revolution against economic justice, in the early years of the 20th Century. This was none other than the advent of communism.

Communism Takes on the World

Communism took on the world during the early years of the 20th century, mostly as a protest against economic exploitation of the labour class. Communism began to develop as a logical economic system that refused to see one man wallowing riches and another rolling in rags, stuck in the swamp of poverty. It can be distinctly understood as a labour movement that shook the world from its roots.

Marxism looked upon history as a series of class-conflicts resulting due to the disparity in wealth and status. Communists felt that the class that controlled the means of production was predominant and denied the rights of the working people who were actually responsible for producing the goods. Those who toiled day and night under adverse circumstances were being exploited and refrained from receiving the value for their work. They were paid a nominal amount whereas the exploiting class, who enjoyed various luxuries of life, was taking the surplus.

The State and the government were also under the influence of the bourgeoisie whereas the labour class was left out in the cold to perish. Hence, it was concluded by the fathers of Communism that history was nothing but the process of evolution initiated by perpetual class struggles.

Marxism proposed an "economy of equilibrium". The idea of the equilibrium was based on the principle that the state must control the means of production and distribute national resources and products evenly among the various classes of the people, irrespective of their status or wealth.

The idea was that individuals must not be allowed "unrestrained freedom"and thereby the opportunity to exploit the means of production for personal gains.

The Renaissance of Japan

After World War II when Japan was nearly devastated owing to the bombings at Hiroshima & Nagasaki, none could imagine that this tiny island would one day startle the whole world with its stupendous progress in every walks of life. Devoid of resources, crippled because of natural calamities and suppressed because of military onslaughts, Japan rose to power due to the sheer patriotism, sincerity and discipline of its citizens.

Here is a story which illustrates the feeling of nationalism that has been the key to its success. There was once a factory in Tokyo manufacturing consumer products and running in losses due to lack of skilled manpower and proper management. Just adjacent to this Nippon factory was situated another factory of competitors who were manufacturing the same products but were enjoying immense profits. The failure of Nippon became all the more glaring because of the convincing success of their competitors dealing in the same products. The workers of the second factory did not feel very happy over the failure of "Nippon" since they knew that "Nippon" is another name for Japan. They could not bear that a factory bearing the name of Japan had to face ignominy owing to losses. They decided to work for another shift - not in their factory but in Nippon. Imagine the workers of a factory devoting their skill, energy and time for rehabilitating the competitor's unit - only because they thought that it was an intrinsic part of Japan! This shows the passionate patriotism of the Japanese. Japan has emerged victorious after weathering many storms and upheavals. It began to open its doors from the 18th Century. Let us glance through the tale of Japanese Renaissance.

The Tale of Japan's Growth

The people of Japan lived in complete isolation since 1641 for a period of 200 years. These years saw stirring changes in the other parts of the world. The feudal system of Japan remained immune to global changes. The emperor enjoyed very little power; **Shogun** was the *de facto* ruler and the head of the warrior class. Although the different classes were constantly at loggerheads with each other, they all maintained their exploitative stance against the peasantry.

Japan tried to maintain peace amidst these conflicts. Some of the great warrior nobles like the **Daimyos** were suppressed. People turned more towards industry, art, literature and religion. Buddhism revived to a great extent. **Shinto** which is the Japanese form of ancestor worship and **Confucianism** (from China) became ideal for the restoration of ethics and morality.

But it was not so easy to remain isolated from change. Feudalism began to spoil the economy. The economic breakdown led to the rise of nationalism.

America began to make repeated attempts to open up Japan in order to have smooth trade with China via the Pacific. In 1853, the first steam ships were seen in Japan and a year later, Shogun agreed to open up two ports.

But there was trouble lying ahead. Shogun began to lose his popularity. People began to revolt against him. In 1867, he was compelled to step down from the throne giving way to Emperor **Mutshihito** who was just a boy of fourteen. He ruled over a period of forty five years from 1867 - 1912 and established the **Meiji Era** meaning **enlightened era**. It was during this period that Japan made advancements and imitated the West in terms of progress. Japan became a great industrial power and to a great extent imperialistic and predatory. Her population increased rapidly. Her ships trotted around the globe. She grew in international eminence.

As is the case with every revolution, this dramatic change in Japan did not go down well with many nobles who were still trying to maintain the feudal system. Their anti-foreign statements began to cause harm to the economy. As a result, the elder statesmen had to chalk out a programme of reform. The older feudal **daimyos** were abolished. The capital of the Emperor was shifted from **Kyoto** to **Yedo,** which later became Tokyo. There were changes in educational, law. Industry grew and a modern Army and Navy came into existence. Japanese students were sent across the globe for acquiring higher education. With all this, also grew the cult of Emperor worship. The emperor neither did away with feudalism nor allowed it to flutter its wings. Japan rapidly westernized herself without destroying her culture. The passionate and self sacrificing patriotism of Japan was evident and closely linked to her progress.

Japan took to Western machinery and industry and with a modern Army and Navy, put on the garb of an advanced industrialized power. But the only problem of Japan was to maintain a balance between new industrialism and old feudalism. In her attempts to manage both, very often her economy went awry. Then began the rise of imperialism in Japan.

The Sino-Japanese War in 1894-95 was a runaway affair for Japan. Her Army and Navy were up-to-date. The Chinese lagged far behind in warfare. Japan won convincing victory over China forcing a treaty on her and putting her on the same level as other Western colonies. China was also forced to secede lands to Japan.

Thus, Japan had triggered off a period of Imperialism in the Eastern part of the world.

The Phenomenal Success of Japan

After incessant struggles and challenges, Japan entered the 20th Century. She became a significant member of the triumvirate force including Germany and Italy. On one side were these three major powers and on the other side were France, England and America. Japan became aggressive and decided to attack Pearl Harbour in America. Although this aggression caused great loss to America, the actual damage was meted out to its ego. America decided to retaliate!

On 6th august 1945 and subsequently on 9th August 1945, America dropped two bombs - one at Hiroshima and the other at Nagasaki. Japan was devastated. From a country deemed to be a world super power, it was almost turned into a debris of ashes. Heaps of corpses lay across the soil. The air resounded with the woes and wailings of orphans and widows. Japan almost stood ruined. But the devastated people of Japan mustered up their lost strength and out of the ashes built up a New Nation which today stands as one of the most advanced and progressive nations in the world.

What are the reasons for the phenomenal success of Japan?

The reasons are:

Patriotism

The people of Japan have an undying love for their nation. For them, their national interests are much above their individual interests. The Japanese know how to safeguard their national pride. They have great respect for public property. Their parks and amusement centres are as well maintained as their own homes. Patriotism is almost their religion.

Discipline

Japan is renowned for her discipline. For Japanese people discipline is not just an imposition of restrictions; rather it is an intrinsic part of work culture. Japanese are seldom late for work, rowdy or unruly. They follow strict self-discipline. Even if they have to protest, they do so by wearing black badges or by working for extra hours and not by exhibiting crude ways of indignation.

What is discipline?

Discipline is not just adhering to rules and regulations; it is the way one lives appropriately. Discipline comprises any act that ensures the security and progress of fellow human beings. If a person maintains utmost discipline and precision in running a slaughter house, his discipline is just superficial since it defies the very purpose of living a worthy life. Hence in every act, *When* the *What, Where, Why* & *How* of the task are properly planned and defined, it is then that discipline actually comes into being. Discipline begins with morality and ends up with the ways of working.

Only if all the above answers are in the affirmative, you can call yourself disciplined.

To become perfectly disciplined one needs to learn how to tame the senses.

Control Anger
Control Passions
Control Actions

Every thought and deed properly controlled is one act properly performed. If individuals can maintain proper discipline, a society or a nation is bound to be Great.

A person who is disciplined can develop other virtues easily.

There are other reasons for Japan's greatness too:

Confidence

The people of Japan are always confident that they would rejuvenate the destiny of Japan. They are determined to fight all odds and gain the supreme position among the community of Nations.

Honesty

An average Japanese is known for his impeccable honesty. He gives utmost value to work, hence believes in maintaining integrity in his dealings. He is firm on his commitments and nearly perfect in his dealings. The level of corruption is abysmally low, hence they have succeeded in building up an international reputation.

Labour

No great work can be accomplished without hard work. In Japan the labour classes are even more sincere than the ruling classes. It is because of their extreme hard work that Japan today stands as an economic Giant.

These people believe in Team Spirit. With a population of 120 million, Japan has projected a spirit of tremendous hard work, team spirit and sincerity.

Precision

The world almost swears by Japanese precision. They have mastered the art of ***Quality Management.*** It was Japan, which gave to the world the concept of creating Quality circles. Every single product that it manufactures goes through various quality checks. Only after passing through all the quality circles, a product becomes *Zero Defect* and gains acceptance in the Japanese and international markets. They believe in Quality and accuracy. Whatever they do is nearly worked out to the last precision. It is because of their precision that Japan has almost infiltrated the global market with her own products and risen to astounding economic supremacy.

Japan, as we have seen, has astounded the entire world with its stupendous success. We too can make our nation great, but before that, we first have to mould ourselves positively for facing the challenges of the world. Like Japan, we too may be deficient in so many aspects. But if the will is there, the road to greatness will not be that steep. Every person should just know how to knock, where to knock and when to knock - the destiny is always ready to open its doors to the right aspirant.

Not only in the West but also in India, there have been gems of Greatness who have not only tried to revive the lost glory of the country, but also served as beacon lights for the entire humanity. Their entire lives were spent with the sole motive of providing social justice, spiritual wisdom and inner peace to the ailing humanity. These great men who came to this world in Modern times actually triggered off an enlightened revolution. This revolution brought about a sublime awakening amidst the oppressed masses and helped them to follow the part of Righteousness, Equality, Fraternity and Justice. Thus these people have been rightly called the Renaissance heroes of India.

Now, we shall look into the lives of these great sons of modern India who shall always be remembered by mankind.

The Great Sons of Modern India

Raja Ram Mohan Roy

The founder of the Indian Renaissance was none other than Raja Ram Mohan Roy. Born in an orthodox Bengali family, Ram Mohan Roy didn't like the social evils since very childhood. The most prevalent evil practice in those days was that of burning females alive after the death of their husbands—known as **Sati**. The greatest emotional blow came to him when his own sister-in-law, whom he loved very much, was subjected to the barbaric ritual of Sati. After this incident, he left for exile for a period of three years. He learnt many languages and studied contemporary religions. There was a burning desire in him to emancipate the social condition of the country that was under British rule at that time.

Raja Ram Mohan Roy dedicated his life to social reform. He became instrumental in abolishing Sati and elevating the condition of women. He advocated the cause of reforms in every walk of life.

His rational outlook, mental courage and urge for reforms made him the father of social reforms in India.

Dayanand Saraswati

One of the shining stars in the horizon of Indian spirituality was Swami Dayanand Saraswati. Born in a deeply religious family in 1824, Dayanand grew up to embrace humanity in its entirety. The religious orthodoxy of his father and the humanitarian outlook of his mother made him a true devotee of God and faithful to religion.

Dayanand was completely shaken up by three notions:
- Faith in idols
- Detachment from the world and
- Disbelief in rituals and ceremonies.

Dayanand was shaped into a real **Mahatma** (enlightened soul) at the feet of his Guru Swami Virjananda. The Guru explained to him the burden of sin and suffering beneath which the world was getting crushed. Inspired by the teachings of his Guru, Dayananda set out with the mission to redeeming mankind from woe and suffering. During his lifetime, he did not take rest and fought single-handed against all sorts of injustice till he gave up his life for the betterment of mankind.

Dayanand's abstruse learning, captivating powers of persuasion, his strength to penetrate through the impregnable orthodoxy with the knowledge of **Shastras**, his fiery eloquence inspired by righteous resentment and a heart glowing with unselfish love for humanity, transfused his work. It made him flaming and scorching.

Dayanand prescribed five daily duties for a householder which must be followed by all those who intend to march towards a superior life.

- Promising Lord to refrain from harming others
- Providing food to the poor and hungry
- Respecting teachers, elders and useful members of the society
- Welcoming and serving guests
- Keeping the atmosphere clean and soothing by burning fragrant substances

His main teachings were to:
- Raise man from indignity
- Follow the doctrine of the Vedas
- Denounce ritualism and expensive ceremonies and

- Reorganize the caste system on the basis of merit, personal qualification, division of labour and mutual cooperation.

Dayanand Saraswati was to a great extent successful in removing child marriage, Purdah system and untouchability. He established Anglo-Vedic education in almost all the parts of the country.

Swami Vivekananda

Swami Vivekananda was the pioneer in bringing about a cultural synthesis between the East and the West. His motto was to give spirituality to the West and bring economic progress for the East. He realized the fact that India needed bread for the poor and the West needed spiritual and cultural Harmony for their self-preservation. He made this motto the mission of his life.

The transformation from Narendra Nath to Vivekananda stands as an example for every youth. Narendra Nath was the son of a very rich man. But since childhood, he was greatly interested in meditating, praying and giving charity.

The untimely death of his father and the huge debts that his father had taken, led the whole family into financial crisis. He was the eldest in the family therefore, confronted with the problem of sustenance. On one hand was his cringing desire to realize God and on the other, the burden of his family. He was undergoing a terrible mental crisis. He wept for days and nights in search of a solution till he met Sri Ram Krishna Paramhansa. Paramhansa was quite the contrast of Narendra. Unlike Narendra, he was illiterate, rustic and emotional. But he was a true and enlightened devotee of God.

Narendra felt a divine solace at the feet of Paramhansa whom he accepted as his Guru. Narendra realized the essence of spirituality and carved out the mission of his life. He was not destined to weep for a few people but to sacrifice his entire life for the betterment of humanity. He laid down his life on the principle of **Service to Mankind is Service to God.**

With no food to eat, only one pair of clothes to wear and no physical or financial support for a period of 10 years, he finally set foot on the shores of America. He wanted to spread the light of spirituality to the West and restore the dignity of India, which was a slave country. What he wanted in return was modern technology and economic wisdom for India. His fiery speech in the "World Parliament of Religions" at Chicago became a history and thus Swami Vivekananda became known throughout the world. He travelled through the entire world within a period of nine years spreading the message of "Universal Brotherhood, Service to Mankind and the Synthesis of East and the West". He opened centres all over the world and restored the lost pride of India.

Although he left for heavenly abode at the young age of 39, he did a lot for the emancipation of Humanity.

Today, his birth anniversary is celebrated as the National Youth Day in India.

Swami Ram Tirth

Swami Ram Tirth was born in a poor Brahmin family. He was contemplative and intelligent even as a child. The death of his mother when he was hardly a few days old and the abject poverty of his family had a deep impact on the life of this great man. He grew extremely concerned and sensitive to the problems of ordinary mankind. His early education under a pious and religious man developed deep sympathies for the concern of mankind and the realization of truth.

He worked extremely hard in his studies and succeeded in becoming a professor of mathematics. His meeting with

Swami Vivekananda was the turning point of his life. He began to follow the footsteps of Vivekananda.

He proved to the world that the greatest benefit lies in imitating great men. Those who remain in the company of pious and holy men, imbibe great virtues. Even our Scriptures have laid emphasis on "Satsang" which means "company of saints and pious souls". This is primarily because holy men emit positive, divine and powerful vibrations that are capable of transforming the life of every ordinary person. Every man who has attained greatness has sought the blessings of a "Guru" or a "Holy teacher".

Ram Tirth began his mission as a spiritual soldier. He like Vivekananda toured the world, talking about the greatness of Indian spirituality and the significance of religious tolerance. Being a humanist, he gave the greatest importance to the problems of man rather to discussions about God. He urged man to see the image of "God" in every living creature and serve them as a service to the Lord.

He was a diehard patriot and identified himself heart and soul with the cause of his motherland. He felt that the suffering of his country or any other country was not a national but an international problem, since suffering was a crime against humanity that every person and nation must strive to remove.

Swami Ram Tirth only lived for 33 years but his life has become an example for millions of young people who want to accomplish something worthwhile in life.

Chapter Three
Cultivating Self-confidence

"I think somehow we learn who we really are and then live with that decision."

F.D. Roosevelt

The Psychic Influence at Birth

It is very true that whatever we achieve in life is directly based upon what we think since our very inception. This process of grasping facts from the external environment, analyzing those facts and eventually assimilating them within us begins even before our birth. Science reveals that the child begins to form attributes even when he is in the womb of his mother. That is why pregnant women are advised not to see violence, vulgarity or anything which is immoral. Rather they should engage themselves in reading good books and scriptures, and in prayer and devotion and with the activities that are moral and warranted. We are bound to reap what we sow.

Can we expect to get mangoes by sowing the seeds of grapes? It is never possible. Therefore, the parents have to be extremely careful with the upbringing of their children especially during the first 5 years of the child's life. If the foundation becomes strong, the future may be ensured.

The attributes of fear, insecurity, lust and anger begin to sprout up right from the first couple of years.

At the time of birth, the child is tied up with the umbilical cord of the mother. While actually coming into this world, the child is separated from the mother simply by cutting this cord. This is for the first time that the child undergoes the act of pain. if the doctor is not careful and the pain is little sharp, the child is bound to develop traces of fear. Such children are more insecure as compared to the others.

The second factor, which proves to be instrumental in moulding the psyche of children, is his upbringing in the first three years. It has been seen that children who are breastfed are more secure and healthy as compared to children who are not. Hence, it is natural for the child to experience the closeness of his mother before opening his eyes. It is also quite true that children till the age of 3 are most receptive to new things. They tend to grasp almost everything, which they see or feel. During this phase, the children must be exposed to colours, natural beauty and acts of kindness such as feeding and patting animals, caressing younger brothers and sisters, sharing toys etc. People who are destined to achieve greatness exhibit a keen sense of enquiry and sensitivity at this age. These are the formative and educative years for a child, which most elders tend to overlook. Children who are overtly protected grow up to be timid. On the other hand children who are not given ample care become harsh and sometimes insensitive to others.

Children till the age of 5 have a highly emotive nature. They are very much aware of their surroundings. The relationship between parents proves to be a vital factor in the mental and emotional make-up of a child. Parents who are always quarrelling bitterly in front of their child are directly responsible for spoiling the child's future. Therefore, it is absolutely necessary for a child to get a cordial ambience where he can bloom.

Children are extremely sensitive to sounds and pictures. Blaring noise and loud sounds can adversely affect the mind of the child. He can become mentally weak, irritable and sometimes even violent. Viewing vulgar movies and pictures can also have a detrimental effect on the mind of a child. Mothers who expose themselves to the electronic media during pregnancy may ruin the general health and mental make-up of the child.

From birth to adolescence, the best school is the mother's lap. The child should not be sent to school till the age of 5, instead he should be encouraged to be with nature and discover the world with his own eyes. This concept of ***discovering by one's self***, needs encouragement and due implementation. As we have discussed before, nature is indeed the best teacher. If we want to learn about the birds and the bees, what better place can we find other than the lap of nature?

Hence, during and after the birth of a child, he must be kept away from the following:

- *Noise*
- *Pollution*
- *Violence*
- *Media and*
- *Computers*

The child should be exposed more and more to the following:

- *Colours*
- *Plants & Trees*
- *Birds & Animals*
- *Devotional songs*
- *Fresh Air*

If infancy is well managed, the child is almost ready to welcome adolescence.

The Years of Adolescence

The years between 10 and 17 are the most significant years of a person's life. The period of adolescence as it is called, is the formative period, when man can either make his life or break his life. During these years, a youngster is full of zest and energy. If this energy is not given the right direction, it tends to lose its way. The energy needs an outlet - either by way of physical activities or by way of mental activities. When the students start complaining of pressure and workload, their problem needs to be eased out with the help of sports, various types of performing arts, mass communication and social activities. It is indeed very difficult for individuals to change the education system or even avoid it, but it is always possible to carve out a parallel stream of education for the healthy development of the child.

This brings us to the question - *What kind of education is required for imbibing the virtues of greatness?*

The Ideal Education

In the words of Swami Vivekananda **Education is not the amount of information that is stuffed into your brains and runs riot there all through your life. Education must be man making and character building.**

Education is quite distinct from literacy. Merely by cramming up facts and figures, a man cannot call himself educated. It is better to instil five virtues and to live upon them with heart and soul than to learn by heart almost a whole library. If we look into the lives of great men and women, we will find that it is not bookish knowledge that has made them great. Rather it is their experience and understanding of truth that has made them great. There have been innumerable people who did not get the opportunity to get higher education, but their whole life was rich and colourful because of their rich experience and other qualities. One such person was James Watt.

James Watt

The harnessing of the steam power has been one of the

greatest inventions in the field of science and the man who brought about this great invention is none other than James Watt.

As a child he showed no potential and his indolence annoyed his parents. At the tea table his aunt used to chide saying, "James, I never saw such an idle boy as you are; take a book or employ yourself usefully; for the last hour you have not spoken one word, but taken off the lid of the kettle and put it on again, holding now a cup and now a silver spoon over the steam, watching how it rises from the sprout, catching and counting the drops it falls into." Later it was proved by the scientists that as he intently poured his thoughts on the boiling kettle and the steam, he was actually working on the theory of ***Thermodynamics.***

Watt kept on observing, discussing and contemplating on facts. One Sunday morning, while he was taking his constitutional after church, he hit upon a great idea which made him the father of the Industrial Revolution. The boiler was too small to operate an engine; therefore the engine was wasteful in the consumption of steam. The solution was to produce an engine consuming less steam.

James Watt was known for his unfailing concentration. He knew how to stick to a particular task over an extended period of time till he got the results. Not only this, he was also inclined towards humanitarian considerations. James Watt refused to develop his engine by the use of high-pressure steam. He thought that it would endanger public life by causing explosions.

Till the end of his life, he continued his obsession for inventions. He stuck to whatever he thought. And that became the reason for his success.

Rabindra Nath Tagore:
The Epitome of Education

The Wakeful ageless God Calls today on our soul- the

soul that is measureless, the soul that is undef(
soul that is destined to immortality and yet
soul that lies in the dust.

These few lines written by Tagore show the exaltation of his thoughts, the essence of his spirit and the truth of present conditions. In these lines, he has in fact given the wisdom of the entire world.

Rabindra Nath Tagore was born on May 6, 1861 in Bengal in an elite Hindu Family. He was the youngest son in his family. During his childhood, he was brought up with discipline. But all attempts to send him to school failed. Rabindra Nath felt choked in the confines of school. He felt that it cramped his spirit of independence, his creativity and imagination. He enjoyed studying in the natural beauty of his garden, which infused a sense of serenity and harmony. Private lessons were imparted to him at home. He came in contact with cultured, thoughtful and educated people who were close family acquaintances.

Once as a small boy, he went to the Himalayas along with his father. The soothing atmosphere and the close company of his learned father intensified his sympathetic and mystical temperament. The early knowledge of the **Upanishads** that he received from his father made him develop a spirit of Universal love and brotherhood. His elder brothers and women in the family gave him ample encouragement in developing Self-confidence.

On September 20, 1877, he went to England for the first time with the purpose of studying Law. He returned to Bengal with novel ideas in religion, literature and politics. Rabindra Nath's strong upbringing made him evolve a highly imaginative, sublime and thoughtful mind. He composed some of the best poetry of all times.

The year 1901 was the milestone in his life. It saw the foundation of Shantiniketan, an International University on the lines of forest schools or **Gurukuls** of Ancient India. The idea was to expose the students to natural surroundings instead of closed confinements and to enable them to develop a free and universal spirit. He strongly believed in the inculcation of creativity and mysticism instead of a cold and calculative mind. Here in his school he wanted to develop perfect world citizens.

In 1903, Rabindra Nath was awarded the Nobel Prize for **Gitanjali**. Later on, it was followed by his knighthood. But due to the Jallianwala Bagh massacre in 1919, Rabindra Nath Tagore, exhibiting sublime love for his country, relinquished his knighthood.

Rabindra Nath Tagore gave the message of extreme compassion, tolerance, universality and patriotism to the world. His greatness lies in the fact that his childhood and adolescence were utilized in gaining true knowledge alloyed with the gems of supreme spirituality and openness.

The years between eleven to seventeen are extremely important for every individual. This is the period when a person undergoes many physical, mental and emotional changes. An adolescent must be dealt with extreme care for from this stage onwards, he can either go towards the heights of success and glory or fall into the abyss of ruin and destruction. Therefore, it is necessary to know about the problems during adolescence.

Problems During Adolescence

During adolescence a child can face various problems. This is the period when a boy or a girl steps into the threshold of adulthood. The child undergoes immense emotional turbulence. It is during this period that the raw energies must be converted into creative activities. The emphasis should be on the holistic development of the child rather than on academic development only.

The problems generally faced are complexities, evil company, feeling of inferiority or lack of confidence and sometimes superiority complex.

Complexities

Complexities arise when a person becomes conscious of what others think or feel about him. Instead of concentrating on his work, he begins to concentrate on others. Children who lack a proper family, sound guidance and care, develop certain negative complexities whereas children who are too much pampered, develop a positive complex. Both types of complexities can undermine the progress of an individual.

This can be elaborated further. Complexities are of two kinds:

Inferiority & Lack of Confidence

Inferiority complex can be dangerous for a growing individual. Such a person can never work towards greatness. He often commits mistakes in order to hide his own weaknesses.

Superiority Complex

Superiority complex is basically an over-estimation of the self. It can arise because of good looks, earnings, learning or family. A person suffering from superiority complex actually restricts his scope to grow. He begins to feel that he has something more than others. Such people become unpopular among friends and relatives. Although they can feel happy at times, it can never give everlasting joy. Such a complex can become a source of isolation and criticism.

For avoiding complexities, adolescents must be brought up with a sense of equality for all. This is possible only if parents and elders set a proper example before them.

Evil Company

Bad Company is the source of all evil and atrocities. Bad friends are worse than the bitterest enemies. Adolescents learn most things from their friends. If they are not good, habits such as smoking, drugs, drinking or gambling can be learnt. Parents must be completely aware about the kind of friends or company their children keep. There should be no compromise in this regard. Bad Company can ruin the life of an individual. This holds good for persons of all ages.

To remove the above problems, it is necessary to divert the interests of the adolescent towards constructive ends. Students, who are shy, need to be exposed to debating, speaking and singing. Those who suffer from inferiority complex need to develop certain skills that can make them develop their cutting edge over others. Evil company can be avoided only when an adolescent is exposed to good books, a congenial family atmosphere and the inculcation of productive hobbies such as gardening, reading, playing musical instruments etc.

But the greatest problem that confronts an adolescent is to match his desires with the desires of his parents. The difficulty actually arises if John wants to become a writer but his parents want him to become an engineer. Such confrontations give rise to frustrations, depression and stress.

Many great men and women have been confronted by similar situations, but they could find an answer to them.

Always a Winner

There are some people in the world who are **Born to win**. Their mental courage and confidence always make them face every storm. Although they may fail in one task or another, their greatness continues to live even after their death. Nothing comes in the path of their mission. Neither the barrier of age, nor of sex, colour, creed, caste or wealth. One such Person who almost stands apart in the history of Britain is **Horatio Nelson**.

Horatio Nelson - The Born Winner

The entire way was filled with snow and it was almost dangerous to travel through the wild paths of eighteenth century Norfolk. The way was a narrow road across a marshland. A young boy of twelve was going to school with his brother William. They were asked to return home because walking in the snow could prove fatal. The young boy refused to return. His honour was at stake. He preferred death to retreat. He continued moving forward. They finally reached the deep drifts of snow which made their way extremely difficult. William thought it safe to return. But his brother simply refused. "We must go on", he said, "remember, it was left to our honour." That boy eventually reached home with his brother William. When his grandmother enquired whether he was fearful, he asked "What is fear?" The boy was none other than Horatio Nelson.

Horatio Nelson was the sixth member in a family of eleven. He was a sickly child. But he possessed unparalleled mental strength. His father was a country priest and his mother was a very pious lady. His parents were extremely poor. When he was hardly nine years old, his mother died. At the tender age of twelve he joined the Navy when cruelty, intoxication, whipping, revolt and murder were the regular features of Sea-life.

Nelson was so poor and weak that people thought that he would perish at sea. However, he succeeded in overcoming his physical weakness merely by determination. He never wanted to lose any task he undertook. And even if he did, he never accepted defeat mentally. He did those things which others never dared to do. Once he stole some apples from a garden and gave them to his friends saying that he did so because others were afraid to do so. In this attitude lies the secret of Nelson's greatness—to do what others do not dare to do.

Nelson always possessed a keen desire to be adventurous. He managed to get himself appointed in the ship Seahorse, which was proceeding towards the East Indies but within two years he became seriously ill and was compelled to return home. Ill-health brought him severe depression. Nelson became thoroughly despondent. He was undergoing a severe mental crisis when all of a sudden, out of his mental agony, a fire was kindled within.

He took a vow of dedicating his life for his country and the King. "I will be a hero, and confiding in Providence, I will brave every danger."

That was the commencement of his journey towards greatness and self-confidence. Many a time he moved into the jaws of death and weathered the gravest storms. His mental courage gave him the strength to shake the roots of death itself.

Nelson, who was once a frail boy became a great Admiral. He went through the tough school of experiences and finally emerged victorious, but he always remained soft from within. He was always warm and generous; he never forgot the hardships that he faced and always inspired his junior officers. He never forgot his friends, never ceased to exhibit compassion. Whenever he had any opportunity, he would always help others. And above all he was filled with glowing patriotism, an unfathomable desire to do his best for his country, England.

❑❑

Chapter Four

Churning Out A Great Personality

The Personality Traits of Great People

Great people always possess certain matchless qualities which others don't have. What are those qualities? Let us try to find them out.

All great people have many traits in common. Among these, there are certain qualities that are inborn and certain which can be imbibed. To inculcate a quality or an attribute, it needs a strong desire, continuous practice and regular improvisation. A player cannot attain perfection unless he devotes himself to regular practice. Similarly a musician has to be with his instrument almost all the time. It takes years and years of hard work to nurture a good quality or a skill.

The common personality traits of all great people are:

Lofty Ideals

The first and foremost sign of greatness is exalted thoughts. People who are not supported by high ideals can achieve momentarily success but cannot sustain their success for a very long time. One with a bad motive gets exposed very easily, as we see the trend with today's politicians. Although they do possess many qualities of the head, but when it comes to the heart or the soul, they are found to be opportunists. Whatever path one chooses towards greatness, he should always try to enjoin it with the greater interests of mankind. The more people benefit from your work, the better it is for you. Therefore, one must fill one's mind with Great Ideals and out of that great work will come out.

Dharma

"**Dharma**" or Virtue is one of the ingredients to churn out the flavour of Greatness. There have been innumerable people in this world who have defeated enemies, acquired wealth, enjoyed fame and wielded power but very few have conquered and ruled over the hearts of millions. To rule over hearts needs a single virtue. It is dharma. You may or may not possess a great personality or be endowed with riches, but if you have "Dharma", you will surely complete your journey towards Greatness.

"Dharma" consists of the five fold paths:

Compassion: Towards the poor, the old, the weak, the handicapped, children, women and animals.

Charity: Feeding the hungry, treating the diseased and teaching the unlettered.

Truth: Being truthful and honest in thought, word and deed particularly at the place of work and worship.

Devotion: Devotion to God, to the Guru and towards knowledge and work.

Chastity: To maintain one's personal aura, it is very important to maintain chastity in thought, word and deed. A person intending to become great must have control over what he thinks or says. He must strictly adhere to the five spokes of control, which are: controlling Mind, Speech, Tongue, Sex organs and Hand.

The world has given many apostles of "Dharma". But one name that almost shines like a pole star in the sky of Greatness is that of Ashoka.

Ashoka the Great–An Apostle of Dharma

Ashoka, first of the Great rulers in India to emerge as a legend from the mists of hoariness and tradition, left to us a mindboggling series of epitaphs carved upon pillars and rocks across the States of India. They disclose a lover of virtue and compassion, of gentleness and humanitarianism, of benevolence and magnanimity. Ashoka stands alone in history, as a King having ruled a great empire and conquered millions of hearts. He did not accomplish his Greatness by the edge of a sword rather used the weapon of Love and Piety with an unwavering regard for the sanctity of human life. He impregnated his empire with all the virtuous tenets of Buddhism and in doing so, ensured the dissemination of this religion to far flung countries specially in the Eastern world. A man of deep intellect, mercy and strength of character, he ranks among the greatest men of the world, not only by virtue of what he did but mainly of what he was. He inherited the throne from his father Bindusar in 273 B.C.

The Great Transformation

In the initial years of his rule, Ashoka behaved like an autocrat. His favourite pastimes were hunting, feasting and war. Thousands of animals were slaughtered everyday for his royal feasts.

He was almost the undisputed emperor of India but his eyes were fixed upon the small Kingdom of Kalinga (Orissa) that refused to give in to the ambitious appetite of Ashoka. Ashoka was absolutely determined to annex Kalinga to its vast empire.

The war began. It was one of the fiercest battles to have taken place in India. The soldiers of Kalinga fought valiantly. The result of the war was appalling. One lakh people were slain and one lakh fifty thousand were captured in the terrible war. Thousands of people were wounded, innumerable children became orphans and one lakh women were widowed.

It is said that when Ashoka visited the battle-ground, he was struck with a deep sense of remorse and anguish. The effect of the mass slaughter made a profound impact on his mind. This was the turning point in the life of Ashoka.

One of the greatest conquerors in the history of mankind became one of the greatest humanitarians the world has ever witnessed.

One of the rock edicts erected by Ashoka says, "His majesty feels remorse on account of the conquest of Kalinga, because during the subjection of a previously unconquered country, slaughter, death and imprisonment of people necessarily occur, whereat his majesty feels profound sorrow and regret."

Immediately after the war of Kalinga, Ashoka embraced Buddhism. After practising the practical aspects of Buddhism for a period of two years, he commenced his "Law of Piety."

The Law of Piety

One of the edicts summarizing the essence of Ashoka's Law of Piety says :

The Law of piety, to wit, obedience to father and mother is good, liberality to friends, acquaintances, relatives, Brahmins and ascetics is good, avoidance of violence and extravagance & violence of language is good.

Ashoka tried to establish the rule of love and peaceful existence. In place of huge provisions of animal flesh before the Kalinga war, the royal kitchens were restricted to the preparation of meat of one deer and two peacocks everyday.

The Royal edict dealing with the purity of life states :

Formerly in the kitchen of his majesty King Priyadarshan each day many thousands of living creatures were slain to make curries. At the moment, when this pious edict is being written, only these three living creatures, namely two peacocks and one deer are killed daily and the deer not invariably. Even these creatures shall not be slaughtered in future.

Ashoka even restricted the people from catching fish and hunting innocent animals. Ashoka took concrete steps to ensure that his Law of Piety was implemented. One of his most innovative moves was the appointment of the censors of Piety who would see that Piety was properly followed at all places. Kalinga rock edicts mentions about the duties of the officials to the bordering tribes. It states: **Do your duty and inspire these folk with trust so that they may be convinced that the king is unto them even as a father and that, as he cares for himself, so he cares for them, who are as the King's children.**

He believed in the transformation of the people rather than their repression. He continued saying, **There are however certain dispositions which render success impossible namely envy, lack of perseverance, harshness, impatience, want of application, idleness, indolence. You should therefore desire to be free from dispositions, inasmuch as the root of all this teaching consists in perseverance and patience in moral guidance.**

He expected his subordinates to act in accordance with his principles. He said

I have accordingly arranged that at all hours and in all places—whether I am dining or in the ladies's apart-

ment, in my bedroom or in my closet, in my carriage, or in the palace gardens—the official reporters shall keep me constantly informed of the people's business, which business of the people I am ready to dispose of at any place.

And in a different passage from the same edict, it said:

Work I must for the public benefit—and for what do I toil? For no other end than this, that I may discharge my debt to animate beings, and that while I make some happy in this world, they may in the next world gain heaven.

Ashoka reigned for a period of forty years. During these four decades, not only did he appoint the "Censors of Piety", he also put into practice the principles that he ordained. He established a wide network of road communications throughout his empire, planted huge banyan trees on either side of the roads, erected free rest-houses for the travellers at frequent intervals and also established hospitals in almost every district.

Everywhere on behalf of King Ashoka, two remedies were arranged. One for the men and the other for animals. Herbal & Medicinal Plants were imported and planted wherever necessary. Wells were even dug for the use of passers-by wherever necessary.

Throughout the vast empire no King has ever been able to rule with so much of righteousness and compassion ensuring complete peace and freedom of his people. Although many personalities have grown in power and position but no monarch has, till date, been able to match the Greatness of Ashoka. It was "Dharma" that propelled him to develop confidence within himself and achieve greatness.

The other significant personality trait that all great men and women must possess is Charisma. Charisma can be inculcated if one strongly wills. Let us first underst[and] charisma is?

Charisma

Charisma is basically the capability of a person to attract others. It can either be with appearance or behaviour or mannerisms depending upon the atmosphere and the situation. A charismatic personality stands apart from the crowd. He can be easily identified in the crowd. His face is radiant, his appearance is aesthetic, his mannerisms are sophisticated and most importantly, he exudes a positive aura which makes him look different.

Develop an aura

Every person has an aura or a halo around him. This comprises the rays that emit from a person's body. When a person is full of divine thoughts, he emits yellow or white rays. If he is angry, the rays turn red. A person who is gloomy or has an evil temperament begins to throw out black rays. These rays have a deep impact on the atmosphere. Wherever the person goes, or whoever comes in contact with him gets influenced by these rays. A man emitting yellow and white rays begins to attract people. He wins the favour of others, wherever he goes. Similarly, a person giving out black rays begins to repel others. He becomes unpopular and confronts failures. This aura can be measured in quantitative terms. Great people, particularly saints and sages may develop an aura up to several kilometres. Whoever comes within that range, cannot escape the magnetism of that person.

There are certain ways to develop that aura. These ways are-

- The inculcation of pious, virtuous and dynamic thoughts
- Practising meditation on some beautiful deity or ideal

- Eating healthy food and avoiding non-vegetarian diet. A person who eats non-vegetarian food emits uneven waves
- Conservation of energy by avoiding all types of indulgences
- Being in the company of holy people
- Control over passions, anger and fear.

Keep a smiling countenance

A smile is a shield which conceals a thousand storms appearing in your heart. It costs nothing but spreads happiness. A glum face can never be successful in attracting people. Your thoughts are directly responsible for your deeds. Gloominess can attract nothing other than gloominess. Some people become disturbed at the slightest provocation. They either become depressed or irritated. Their negative thoughts create negative vibrations in the atmosphere as a result of which failure ensues. To avoid this, try to overlook trifle matters and imbibe pleasant thoughts within you, which can only spread happiness around you. A man who attains greatness tries to give joy to others. He knows how to conceal his sorrow with a smile and never lets depression or sadness settle in his heart for a long time. For, he has no time to waste. For him every moment is precious for the accomplishment of his thoughts.

Have an aesthetic appearance

To create an initial impression, it is important to emphasize on the physical appearance as well. For that it is necessary to remain clean, well dressed and poised. Loud talking, guffawing, shabby clothing and unkempt hair can reduce the charm of the personality.

The Magnetic Aura of Great Leaders

Many personalities have moved across the modern world

stage with a more stunning thrive and a greater aplomb than Mahatma Gandhi; though few have had so much influence on the history of our times. With a fragile and scrawny body, and with few of the traditional qualities of leadership, but gifted with a clear vision and resolute faith, this remarkable man awakened in oppressed people a sense of self-esteem and a pledge to strive for their independence. His long struggle on behalf of the Indians in South Africa and his emergence later as a prophet in the hearts of millions of his fellow-countrymen; his political sagacity and legal insight enabled him to translate his faith into effective action. Above all he won world renown by his doctrine of Non-Violent resistance. In the lap of poverty, he spent his life in service. His achievement, rare if not unique was to bring to politics the moral face of a great religious leader. He was an "apostle of truth", a messiah of the downtrodden and the silent voice of India. He was rightly called Mahatma - the Great Soul and he really proved it to the world.

From Mohandas to Mahatma

Mohandas Karamchand Gandhi was born on October 2, 1869 at *Porbandar* in Gujarat (India). When in school he was bashful, timid and average in studies. Nobody could ever feel that there was a great soul lurking within the slim frame of his.

One night, during 1893, when a lawyer boarded the first class compartment of a train to Pretoria in South Africa, he was forcibly thrown out of the compartment for being an Indian. He was compelled to sit outside with the driver and assaulted and beaten by the conductor. This incident almost became the turning point in the life of that man since he was none other than M.K Gandhi. From there began the journey towards greatness..... the transition from Mohandas to Mahatma. His life is an epoch of greatness buttered with truth, non-violence and humanity.

But the saga of freedom began with his work in South Africa. When in Natal (South Africa), the Indians and South Africans were subjected to a life of utter disgrace and humiliation, he rose as an Apostle of Justice. The freedom movement had begun and Gandhi was the torchbearer. In 1896, Gandhi came to India for a period of six months. He delivered lectures, issued pamphlets and held public meetings highlighting the condition of Indians in Natal. This triggered a series of protests by Europeans in Natal. On his return to Natal, Gandhi was subjected to threats and physical assaults. He had to bear the fury of angry mobs, but his journey for freedom and justice continued.

Inspite of his struggle at Natal, his heart ached for his motherland, bled for his brethren and wept as a protest against injustice meted out to Indians. He returned to India. Seeing his opulent Motherland shackled in the chains of slavery and his fellow-countrymen leading a life of abject penury, he left all that he had earned and never cared to look back. **He had just one mission in his life - Freedom of India.** He began to lead a saintly life - away from all worldly passions and focused his mind on the liberation of his Motherland. His sublimity, purity and devotion to God enhanced his magnetism. He developed a unique aura that captured almost the whole of India. The weapons that he used to bring about this conquest were love, truth and peace.

His battle for freedom began from *Champaran* in Bihar, where the peasants were oppressed under the system of indigo plantation. He faced stiff opposition from the landlords and the government. This struggle brought him face to face with the poverty and backwardness of the villages and he became increasingly occupied with the regeneration of the peasants.

From *Champaran,* he passed to *Khaira* to aid the peasants there in their revolt against the government assessment of their crops after a bad harvest. Although the struggle met with moderate success, Gandhi had already become a phenomenon in India.

A few years later came the first great Civil disobedience movement against the Rowlatt Act. It met with unprecedented success.

With his agitation for ***Swaraj*** he also continued his movement towards social reforms. He motivated and gathered the women folk to protest against liquor. He also coined the name ***Harijan*** meaning the ***children of the Lord*** to give due respect to the so-called lower castes and to remove the problem of untouchability. He went as far as adopting an untouchable girl as his own daughter. He also initiated the boycott of foreign goods in order to prevent their use.

Gandhi continued his resistance against British Empire with his various movements. The Non-Cooperation Movement followed by Civil Obedience Movement, Salt *Satyagraha,* and last but not the least Quit India Movement shook the nation from its deep slumber. India was on fire with the spirit of nationalism and the man who ignited this fire was none other than Gandhi whose weapon was was non-violence. His only aim was not the freedom of India rather the establishment of an utopian India. Gandhi went to jail several times but none could undermine his spirits. He had given himself up to the cause of his motherland. Let us briefly examine Gandhi's personality traits.

The qualities that brought about the transition from Mohandas to Mahatma are:

A definite purpose

Mahatma Gandhi had a single purpose in his life and that was the *Freedom of India* through the right means. He sacrificed his family, career and all the luxuries of his life for accomplishing his mission.

If you are having a definite purpose in life, ask yourself - what things can I sacrifice for achieving my goal? If there is almost everything, apart from morality, character and compassion that you can sacrifice, you are surely towards your path to success.

Love of truth

The most startling feature that distinguished Gandhi from other great people was his unwavering love of Truth and Justice. He never even supported the unjust cause of his own country. All of a sudden, he had called off the Non-Cooperation movement when he realized that the people were not complying with peace and Non-Violence. He gave as much importance to the means as to the end.

If you want to ride the crest of greatness, never yield before untruth. Be bold to say what you feel and intend to achieve. If you feel hesitant to talk about your mission and there is something that you do not want to reveal, it either means that you are not confident of your mission or that your mission lacks sublimity. Always try to support Truth, even if it goes against you.

Tenacious determination & confidence

Mahatma Gandhi stood like a rock before the mighty British Empire. Nothing could sway him from his path. He met with innumerable struggles and failures... he spent several years of his life behind bars, he faced the assaults of Britishers, underwent countless humiliations, remained without food and water for days, sacrificed the happiness of his family, lost his health and wealth, but he kept fighting. Gandhi has taught to the world "the art of being determined".

A man who is willing to achieve success has to be prepared to burn in the fire of ordeals. A block of iron can only be turned into a shining sword by burning it in scorching fire. Raw gold can only be adorned into a beautiful ornament by consigning it to heat. Similarly, an ordinary man can only achieve greatness after breaking every barrier, which comes on his way.

You break the wall, don't let the wall break you!

Confucius

Loyalty, benevolent authority and dutiful submission as well as courtesy, chastity, abhorrence of violence, with the Golden Rule "What you do not want for yourself, do not do to others". That was the fundamental principle of Confucianism, the ethical code, which for centuries swayed the soul of China. Confucius, the sage, teacher and reformer, whose wisdom and virtue gave birth to the movement that has taken his name, died in the fifth century before Christ, but his name continues to live even today.

It was in the winter of around 551 B.C that Confucius was born in the state of Lu in China as the son of a commandant. The Chinese fables say that when Confucius was born, dragons and nymphs appeared, his mother heard sweet strains of music. On the baby's body were found forty nine marks and the words "He will originate Principles and settle the affairs of men." The cave where he was born saw a tablet inscribed "The son of the essence of water shall succeed to the withering Tsow and become a Throneless King."

More than these lovely fables is the fact that Confucius at a very early age, gave clear signs of extraordinary ability. The death of his father when he was barely three gave a serious blow to the financial condition of his family as a result of which, he began to earn his living since the very childhood. But inspite of his poverty, his mind was deeply inclined towards learning and only at the tender age of fifteen, he was determined to become a sage.

Although Confucius married at the age of nineteen and had children, he was extremely conscious of the dual combination - to become not only a learned man but also a wise ruler. At the age of twenty-two, he began his career as a teacher and sage by founding an academy or school in which he expounded the principles of right conduct and government. His students were very young. He collected considerable fees from those who were rich and the poor were given education without having to pay. None was turned down on account of being poor. Ability and devotion were the only criteria by way of which he judged his students. "When I have presented one corner of a subject and the pupil himself cannot learn the other three, I do not repeat the lesson."

His reputation grew both as a teacher and an administrator. As an official, he came to be known as zealous reformer who never hesitated to attack archaic norms and as a scholar, he mastered the subjects of history and philosophy till the age of thirty. He always stood firm in his conviction having studied exhaustively the facts and figures of the past and having strong principles about the government as well as ethics.

In 517 B.C. two young men of high rank in the state of Lu became his ardent disciples and along with them Confucius visited the capital of the empire, where he continued his historical research in the imperial library, and studied music which he was passionately fond of. Music played a vital role in his life. Not only did it divert his attention from different things of interest but also made him realize that it was an important instrument for restoring things to their equilibrium. He went on to make music an intrinsic part in his idea of Governance.

It was during this period that he met Lao-Tse, who was adverse in character but similar in greatness and founder of Taoism, one of the greatest religions in China.

Confucius was practical, business-like, earthly minded and a rationalist. He believed in the sedulous cultivation of virtue. He believed ethics and virtues to be the most befitting instrument for expressing spiritual perfection.

Confucius hated the oppressiveness of Government. He was deeply moved by the story of a woman whose husband was killed by a tiger; then again her son fell a victim to the tiger, yet she refused to quit that place because it did not have an oppressive government. Confucius is said to have remarked, "an oppressive government is fiercer than a tiger."

According to his disciples, Confucius was exquisitely precise and courteous in his mannerisms. He was punctilious to a great extent in all his work as well as religious observances. At the age of fifty-two, he was appointed the governor of the city of **Chung-tu** and later on assumed the highest offices of the state. With the help of his uncanny genius as well as with the support of his disciples a mal-administered government vanished into thin air. Corruption and dishonesty hid their heads; truth, faith and honesty became the common principles of men and the women became docile and virtuous. He was an idol of his people and was beautifully captured in their fables, songs and hearts.

Confucius was very advanced in many of his reforms. He not only fed the poor directly but also made ample arrangements for assigning various kinds of healthy food to the young and the old alike.

He was selective about assigning different tasks to the people according to their physical and mental ability. He fixed the prices of goods and used state revenue for the development of trade. Communications got a face-lift, roads and bridges were improved. The powers of the nobles were curbed and common man found freedom from exploitation and oppression. He made all the people equal in the eyes of law. He never even hesitated in attacking the powerful if they dared to go against his reforms.

After his reform activities in LU for a period of three years, Confucius went on to search another land where his reforms could be accepted. He wandered from place to place for a period of thirteen years in search of a place, which he could transform into the land of his dreams. With coarse rice to eat, water to drink and his bended arms for a pillow, he continued his struggle. He never muttered a single complaint. He maintained equanimity in suffering and in times of prosperity. When he had to remain without food for quite some days, his disciple commented, "Must the superior man endure like this?" **"The superior man may have to endure want",** came the reply from Confucius. *"The small man in similar conditions loses his self confidence."* Confucius finally returned to LU and spent most of his time in instructing his disciples. He also wrote a book titled *Ch'un Chi'u King* covering records about the past. He died in 479 B.C. but his fame continued to spread throughout the world.

He never yielded before injustice and possessed a strong ability to endure hardships in order to accomplish what he desired. He never deviated from the path of righteousness. He was too strong to get swayed away by attachments and emotions. These were the characteristics that led him to establish a new religious order in the conservative nation of China .

The Art of Communication & Oratory

A young man was declaiming aloud against the competition of the waves breaking and surf surging back over the stones. They probably thought he was mad. Certainly they could not have believed that they had witnessed the rigorous self-training of one of the greatest orators the world has ever produced - his name was **Demosthenes**.

The classical tradition of Public speaking, which governs the oratory of today as much as it did in the ancient past, leaps from the works of one of the greatest and the noblest of ancient Greeks whose style and art have moulded the rhetoric of nations. He has set an example for all those who lack the art of speaking, who are shy of expressing their thoughts in public or who are suffering from any sort of speech deficiency. His wordy onslaughts still reverberate with patriotism and idealism in the hearts of millions of oratory lovers around the globe.

Demosthenes was born with a bad impediment in his speech, and in his efforts as a boy to control his speech, he twisted his face into quite frightening countenances. His physical handicap could not undermine his spirits and he grew more determined day-by-day to overcome his defect. His physical handicap could never undermine his confidence.

What did he do to overcome his weakness?

To correct the stammering in his speech, he began to speak with pebbles in his mouth; he continued speaking till his mouth bled. He kept staring at a mirror till the distortions in his expressions were removed. To improve his pronunciation and bring more emphasis to his speech, he went on with the most arduous and steep walks where his voice acquired brute strength. Not only this, when the waves clashed violently against the rocks in the wild seas, he declaimed aloud in order to habituate himself with the din of a public assembly. He also confined himself in the subterranean caves, shaved half of his head and devoted himself to educational pursuits. In this quiet withdrawal, by the help of a flickering lamp, he composed the majority of his orations which have been the greatest speeches throughout the history of man.

In 352 B.C., Demosthenes with his burning patriotism and fiery eloquence aroused the slumbering masses of Athens in his first speech which went down in history as the most "hair raising" address to the masses till recent times.

In order to succeed in any field, the art of speaking is vitally essential. Words are capable of creating epochs and causing revolutions. Even to communicate with Gods, we need the medium of words either in the form of prayer or in the forms of mantras & hymns. Therefore, there are some believers in Hindu Philosophy who ardently feel that the entire creation came into existence from a single word. The Greeks also supported this viewpoint by their theory of "Logos". Although we all realize the significance of communication, there are innumerable people in the world, who find speaking to be their biggest lacuna. This section is the life-line for all those people who are strongly possessed by a great mission and have decided to tread the path towards greatness.

Why is the art of communicating so important?

The art of communicating is necessary because :

Everything needs to be marketed

"One who wants to be successful must know the art of selling."

In every task you undertake, you either have to sell products, or ideas, or concepts and last but not the least your own personal charisma. Therefore, words are the cords that tie one person to another. For people who want to make it big in public affairs, it is absolutely necessary to learn the art of ruling the hearts and minds of the people. Words can act like swords as well as like flowers depending upon the speaker and the situation. We must know the art of what to speak, where to speak and how to speak?

How to Develop the Art of Speaking?

Speaking can be broadly categorized into two broad categories:

- *Intrinsic*
- *Extrinsic*

Intrinsic deals with what to speak and extrinsic deals with how to speak. First let us begin with intrinsic:

Develop the will to speak

You can definitely speak if you have the will to. If you are in a party or a get-together, don't be a mute spectator during conversations. Try to participate in conversations to the best of your ability. Do not wait to be questioned rather try to initiate some sort of conversation.

Do not speak about yourself

If you want to develop friends, avoid the letter "**I**". "**I**" **stands as the biggest barrier between people.** Some people have a tendency of narrating their achievements or brooding over personal problems in public. This can irritate people. Nobody wants to hear about you unless he really likes you or unless you become a celebrity. Whenever you are conversing, try to make it participatory. Talk about things that can excite the interest of others. For this you must develop a fair idea about general topics viz. films, music, sports, culture and politics which can ignite the interest of others.

Remain glued to the topic

Whenever you are given a topic, always try to revolve around, only giving yourself the minor liberty of deviating slightly. If you are asked to speak about the latest television programmes, do not start narrating the story of a film that you have recently viewed. Deviating from the topic is the common weakness of most of the people. This problem enhances with age. Try to keep it under check.

Avoid giving personal remarks

Some people derive pleasure in giving critical assessment about others. They love to comment upon how others talk, behave or live. They never hesitate in commenting directly upon the dress or looks of others. This habit can very well offend others. Therefore, one must avoid giving personal remarks.

Make good preparations

You may hardly get a few minutes to prepare your speech. Just after getting the topic, you must jot down the points that you may later on elaborate. Listen intently to what others say. This will help you to get clues for your own speech. Whenever you are asked to speak upon any topic, try to follow the tips given below:

Begin with an example

The topic on which you are asked to speak must begin with an example. You can refer to an article that you have recently read in the newspapers or an incident that you have recently come across. This will make your speech more interesting. For example, if you are required to speak on communalism, you can begin your speech by talking about the communal riots in Bombay in the year 1994 or any such similar incident just in order to arouse public interest. The example that you give can be fictitious but never try to distort facts. This is to say that while talking about yourself or your family, you can give some unoccurred facts but not while talking about historical, geographical, economic or social incidents.

Define the topic

Secondly, you must try to define the topic. The definition may not be scientific but it must have the ability to explain the meaning of the topic to a layman. For example, what is implied by Communalism? You can simply explain it in two words - Religious Discrimination.

Keep the definition brief and self explanatory.

State the consequences

The third step to follow is to speak about the favourable and unfavourable consequences of a given topic. However, there are certain topics that have either advantage or disadvantage only. For example - Communalism. This is such a topic which can have no advantage. Hence it is very important to discuss its ills at length giving valid arguments. On the contrary, if we are asked to speak on Honesty, we can only state the positive features without exception. This will help to give an indepth analysis about the situation.

Explain the prevalent situation

In the fourth step, the current situation pertaining to the given topic must be explained to the best possible accuracy. If you are speaking on communalism, you will be required to state the latest happenings in your city, state and country regarding the same. This information should be based on authentic facts. In case you are not properly informed about the actual condition, then you need not state facts or figures, rather you can restrict yourself to the overall scenario in brief.

Present your own views

In the end, you have to put forth your own views very emphatically. People would be interested in knowing as to what you personally feel about the topic. Not only this, you must express your views as your moral duty towards your audience. Whatever you say must give a clear message and not be merely analytical. Always evoke their thoughts by forcing them to contemplate. This may leave a lasting impression in the minds of the listeners. The speech must always have a pragmatic approach and not something that is beyond the reach of the audience.

Give a multi-dimensional approach to the topic

You can treat each topic in different ways. This treatment may deal with the different view points and conclusions derived from a particular topic.

If you are required to speak on Destiny, you can give several treatments to this topic. You can deal with it philosophically, realistically, literarlly or even scientifically. Destiny can be explained as a mystery, or as a fact or even as scientific misnomer - whichever way suits you. A good orator always exudes utmost self-confidence.

Revealing the Genius within you

Every man has a genius concealed within him,
if he only knew how to manifest it.

How many people must have witnessed the falling apple before, but the only person who could reveal the secrets of Nature from it is **Sir Isaac Newton.**

Sir Isaac Newton

Our knowledge of the Law of Gravitation, the principle by which the entire universe exists, moves and maintains its equilibrium, is the gift of one man - SIR ISAAC NEWTON. To call him the greatest English Scientist & Mathematician would be undermining his contributions to the world of science. At the age of twenty-four, he discovered the principles of Integral Calculus and Binomial Theorem and ten years prior to that, he was merely a farm boy with barely two years at Grammar School to his credit!

Isaac Newton took little interest in his studies. As a child, he was physically weak as a result of which, he was bullied by other classmates. Once, when at Grammar School, a big bully of the class was on the look-out for weaker boys. His obvious choice was Newton. The brawl began and to the utter surprise of the entire class, it was the bully who was knocked off badly by Newton. This incident gave confidence to Newton and he decided to change for the better.

Although Newton gained more confidence in class, he had to confront with bigger problems. His father passed away and he was left alone with his mother to earn their livelihood from a solitary farm. Isaac was forced to quit his grammar school.

Isaac was left with just a single asset - fundamental knowledge of Mathematics. While working in the farm, his appetite for Mathematics grew. But he always regretted the decision of quitting school. Although his mother sympathized with him, she could see no way to help her son. However, his uncle William Ayscough who was a member of Trinity College came to his rescue. Isaac went back to school in 1660 for preparing for College. Although, Isaac Newton was wasting his talents as a farm boy, he was fully aware of his duties as a student. He completely dedicated himself to studies. On June 5, 1661, he was walking confidently in the corridors of Trinity College, Cambridge. In the year 1661, he had already attained his matriculation degree and within three years, he was elected a scholar and graduated in Arts. During the three years of graduation he had mastered almost every mathematical theory of significance. His intellectual capability was almost phenomenal. He fully devoured Binomial Theorem, the principles of Integral Calculus and the methods of calculating the area of curves and the volume of solids. But his most important discovery was the Law of Gravity that he revealed while walking in a garden. Hence, he had established the Law of Gravitation, he had discovered the theorem that the principle governs the existence and movement of the Universe. He was the founder of the Emission Theory of Light and many more.

He was constantly at work trying to reveal the secrets lying hidden. He poured himself into the mysteries of Nature and found immense pleasure in each of his findings. He always tried to quench his insatiable thirst for knowledge. He gave to the world not only the greatest findings in the field of research and science but also the art of self-revelation. If you wish to stand in the ranks of Isaac Newton, you must constantly work upon your intellect, nurture it and give it a tangible shape.

There are innumerable people in this world who want to become successful scientist, astronomer, mathematician or inventor, but they must possess certain important qualities.

The important qualities that are required for all the above professions are:

A Spirit of Inquiry

"Inquisitiveness" or a "Spirit of Inquiry" is the prime most requisite for getting into the above fields. One must have a crying thirst for knowing the unknown, for unraveling the mysteries of nature and an insatiable thirst for knowledge.

Stealing the Hearts of Millions

Since time immemorial, film stars, artists, performers, sportsmen and eloquent speakers have ruled over the hearts of millions. With a single glance, they could win over thousands of people. There are many youngsters who want to make a mark for themselves in the world of showbiz. They always nurture the dream of becoming great artists, entertainers and performers but do not know the right way to approach it. If you are one of them, then there are surely ways to approach your goal. But before aspiring to become an artist or a performer, you must:

Identify Your Talent

You must be very specific with what you want to accomplish. If you wish to become a dancer, focus all your energies towards dancing pursuits. If you want your hobby to become a profession, you will be required to give more time and attention to it.

Practise with Utmost Devotion

Every art needs to be mastered and this can only be possible with continuous practice. Artists who have made it big have spent years in rehearsing and practising. They have sacrificed many significant things in life in order to attain perfection in their field. Every day should be utilized in perfecting the art that you possess.

Maintain Sublimity

Hindus in India believe that any art, knowledge or skill is the gift of Goddess "Saraswati". Hence, performers must always try to maintain sublimity while practising or performing. Bow before the deity before starting your performance, burn incense and camphor in the room where you practise in order to keep the atmosphere pure. Try to practise early in the morning when the atmosphere is apt for gaining knowledge. Rely more upon soothing, fresh and vegetarian food that will help in ensuring your radiance.

Practise Yoga & Meditation

Yoga and Meditation are the sciences that enhance a person's physical and mental vigour and vitality. It gives more stamina, accuracy as well as concentration to a person. Not only this, Meditation also helps in developing personal appeal and magnetism which are significant ingredients for any public figure. Thirty minutes of meditation during dawn and thirty minutes during dusk are said to be ideal to achieve success in any field.

Indulge in Meaningful Art

If you want to become a great performer, never indulge in crap entertainment. Whatever you present must be unmixed with meaningless and lewd performances. Such performances can only give you short-lived name but eventually tarnish your image. Hence, try to work out on your intrinsic value and not just on your external glare.

Be Image Conscious

Although you are more important than your image, your image will follow wherever you go. Once your image is spoilt because of personal or professional reasons, you can rarely restore it. Hence, be extremely careful with your daily habits as well as daily routine.

Avoid Bad Habits

It is seen that people opting for glamorous professions are unable to maintain control over themselves. They begin to indulge in bad habits such as smoking or excessive drinking. As a result of all this, they lose their magnetism which only comes when the energies are properly conserved. Any sort of physical indulgence leads to energy dissipation.

Apart from the avoidance of bad habits and inculcating a dynamic personality, it is also very important to do the right thing, at the right place and at the right time. For this you must follow the right strategy to ensure your success.

In the next chapter, we shall deal with the right strategies required for success and a great life.

❏❏

Chapter Five
Strategy for Building Confidence

What is a Cybernetic Strategy?

Cybernetic Strategy is nothing but proper streamlined approach for undertaking any given task.

Like a war is always won with the help of a properly laid out plan, in the same way any work has to be done with the help of a carefully laid out plan. Similarly, to achieve greatness and nurturing confidence one has to carefully work out the strategy that can almost become a self-propellant for the achievement of success.

As a warrior, a person opting for greatness needs to answer the following questions?

- *What is my target?*
- *What are the major threats?*
- *How to approach the target?*
- *What is the strength of my army?*
- *In how much time do I have to capture the enemy territory?*
- *How will I be able to maintain my victory?*

So, the first step is none other than fixing the priorities.

Prioritizing

Every person has to fulfil various needs in life. These needs can be pertaining to the family, education, career or society. The various needs can be earning a livelihood, taking care of family, maintaining a social image, protest and success and spiritual development etc.

Maslow's theory says that a person first fulfils his physical needs such as food, clothing and shelter, after which he caters to his social needs such as success, name and fame and in the end his spiritual or moral needs. But history bears testimony to the fact that most of the great people dared to break this theory of Maslow's hierarchy and proceeded to set their own priorities. Great spiritual reformers have sacrificed their personal comforts, family and even food and shelter to seek God. They have focused their entire energies on a single priority - to attain divinity! And in spite of all the odds, they have startled mankind by attaining the heights of spiritual powers which was almost inconceivable for the majority of mankind. They have taught to the world to set priorities according to one's strong will and not according to conventional systems, which an average person tends to follow with the fear of social dogmas.

Here, we shall meet a spiritual giant whose priority was to liberate himself and his fellow brethren from sorrow. His name was Siddhartha, later acclaimed as Gautam Buddha.

Gautam Buddha

The entire kingdom was rejoicing the birth of a prince. The palace was overflowing with riches and pleasure. The king and the queen were doting upon the child. But the child's father was lost in his thoughts. He was deeply moved to see the suffering of mankind. Of what use was a son to him who would also be subjected to the old age, disease and death. Why was the life of man subjected to suffering? His mind was violently turbulent in search of truth. And at the dead of night when all retired he rose silently. He saw his little son peacefully resting in the arms of his beautiful wife. He felt a burning urge to clasp the baby in his arms. He managed to curb his impulses. But had he come to the world to be tied down by family ties or was he destined to search enlightenment not only for himself but for the entire humanity?

Leaving all the comforts and pleasures behind him, he set out in search of the Eternal Truth. His priority in life was the quest for Spiritual Truth.

Gautam Buddha began his wanderings across the fertile plains of Ganges till he reached the land in the South. He lived there for six years subjecting himself to rigorous penance and asceticism. He shaved off his head, adorned his body with yellow robes and subjected his body to severe fasts and every recognized form of physical penance. He lived in a forest along with five disciples, exerting through self-discipline the mission of attaining truth.

He came to be known as a pious man, yet he was still oblivious of Truth. His priority in life was not recognition or settling down for mental peace, but to unravel the ultimate spiritual truths. One day, on waking up from a fainting fit produced by his extreme asceticism, a flashing light appeared before his eyes. He realized that physical mortification or extreme fasting was leading him nowhere. He felt the need of preserving his body for achieving his goal. Exhilarated by his realization and a hope for further accomplishments, Gautam wandered through the forests of Gaya in Bihar.

And finally after abiding hour upon hour of splintering mental and spiritual distress, after ranging through every feeling and emotion known to man, from the darkest despair to the brightest hope, Gautam found at last the mission of his life. He became Buddha - the Enlightened One.

He carried out his relentless work against Human suffering and established one of the greatest religions of the world. He ultimately accomplished what he had set his heart to. What he possessed was an unwavering devotion and self-confidence towards his mission.

Planning

Organizing

People who have accomplished Great missions in Life have always been great organizers. They carefully work on the art of motivating and managing people. People who have failed to manage armies, teams or groups have ended up with failures in life. The greatness of a person lies not in moving alone but in carrying along with him people of different mental frame-work. An able organizer always possesses the following qualities:

Tactful

An organizer must be very careful in dealing with colleagues and also subordinates. It is extremely important to keep one's temper mild and be very choosy with words. Harsh words can cause injury not only to personal relationships but also to business dealings. If there is any problem within the organization, it must be nipped in the bud by calling everybody across the table and discussing matters at length. But any sort of rudeness must be avoided as far as possible.

Decision maker

A good organizer is always a prompt decision-maker. He never waits upon crucial decisions for a very long time, rather acts at the right time. An organizer must know what to decide, when to decide, how to decide and most importantly in whose favour to decide. Delays in making decisions can bring losses to an organization.

Manager of contradictions

Where there are several people working, there is bound to be clash of opinions. A good organizer must know how to manage contradictory ideas and persons without being partial. An organization has to consider every viewpoint before deriving conclusions. Moreover, he must remain cool and composed amidst contradictory opinions and should not lose his own equilibrium. Contradictions must be borne with until they are in the best interest of the organization but not beyond that.

Democratic

A good organizer never imposes his own viewpoint forcefully. He rather tries to give an opportunity to each person for exhibiting his talents. A tyrannical organizer cannot survive for a very long time and even if he somehow survives, can never win the admiration and respect of his team members.

Patient

A suitable organizer is extremely patient under all circumstances. If he fails to accomplish a particular task, he does not throw tantrums, rather reviews the entire work, analyses the drawbacks and remotivates the people for further action. He always pursues a task till its successful completion, knows how to keep the adrenaline of his people high.

Receptive

An organizer is always receptive to novel ideas. He keeps himself charged and abreast with changing trends and tries to accommodate his tasks according to the times. He does not keep his mind in a water-tight compartment rather allows the free flow of ideas from all quarters. He is never hesitant to adopt changes and ideas even from subordinates.

Time Scheduling

Apart from organizing, time scheduling is another significant aspect for ensuring success. There is a very old proverb saying "Time and tide wait for no man". Time never waits for man, it is man who has to wait for the right time for doing a work. Man does not know what will happen to him in future. Hence, he has to live every moment to its full.

If you are speeding yourself towards greatness, you must learn the art of proper scheduling.

Prepare weekly schedules for yourself. The schedule must be on the basis of work and not on the basis of time. For example, if you are a student preparing for an examination, you must make up your mind that in one week you have to thoroughly complete three chapters of a particular subject and two of another. On the other hand, if you assign 3.00 p.m to 5.00 p.m for studies but at the end of the week, end up with preparing hardly a couple of chapters, your scheduling will prove to be futile. Hence scheduling must always be task based.

The Significance of Motivation

Apart from a proper management of systems, it is also very necessary to motivate and develop a good temperament.

Every person in this world has a different temperament, a different level of motivation and a different psyche. Therefore, a good organizer or a team leader must be fully conversant with the psyche of his team members and know how to boost their spirits during crisis.

There are mainly two kinds of motivations.

Positive

Positive motivation is meant for all those who possess a soft temperament, especially children and females. It must be adopted by those people who have a predominance of virtues and can be easily motivated. They should be charged with a strong mission, with incentives and accolades. They must be provided help whenever necessary and in times of crisis, they must resort to consoling and inspiring words.

Such people can perform better under pressure. If you regard yourself as one among those, you must seek a noble teacher, a loyal friend and motivating books. This will help you to reaffirm your strength.

Negative

The second kind of motivation which at certain times can be dangerous is suitable for those people who have evil propensities. They are always attracted towards evil. If their pride is wounded and given a proper direction, they can produce wonders. Those who have negative attributes have greater strength to make it big, provided their energies can be fruitfully harnessed. It was easier for Dacoit Valmiki to become a Saint because of the possession of great strength. Negative motivation can include mild punishments or isolation that can make a person realize. However, it can also be dangerous in some cases, especially with children.

Failure or humiliation has also worked as a motivating factor for many people. The renowned poet Kalidas was one of those, who after facing humiliation from his wife, set out on the path of great learning.

Motivation can, however, lead to success only when one learns how to overcome hurdles.

⬜⬜

Chapter Six

Overcoming Hurdles on the Way to Greatness

The Possible Hurdles

In the journey towards greatness and Self-confidence there are many hurdles. If you have decided to proceed on your mission, you must be aware of the possible hurdles that you are likely to face.

What are they?

- *Physical Deformity or Weakness*
- *Poverty*
- *Social Resistance*
- *Lack of Education*
- *Lack of support*
- *Lack of confidence*

  - If physical deformity would be an impediment, the crippled would never have dared to become presidents and rulers. It is the body that becomes deformed and not the mind. Hence, accumulate your soul's force and begin your crusade against this first hurdle. It is not the weight of your body that counts in your journey towards greatness, rather it is the weight of your will that yields results.

  - The riches in the world have been cultivated in the soil of poverty. Rockefeller, Ford & Gates were not nurtured in the lap of wealth. It was the genius within them that enhanced their wealth. The greatest wealth is your confidence which will always help you to overcome the fear of poverty.

- If social criticism is the hurdle, then it is apt to believe that- "Those who can do, cannot criticize."

  If you have a mission, be prepared to face the brickbats because no great work has ever been accomplished without condemnation.

- If you do not possess a respectable degree to boast of, never be daunted. It does not require a maze of intricate information to solve the simple problems of life. To spread love, harmony, peace and wisdom, what you need is a pounding heart and not a convoluted mind.

- If you feel that you are alone in your mission, you are surely living with a wrong conception. If you really believe in God, you can never be alone. In every moment of your life, always feel the living presence of God, Who always supports those who dare to give up their life for a generous cause.

People who believe in their mission never get intimidated by hurdles, for they have a deadly certitude about the truth of their mission.

Socrates

Born in 469 B.C., an ugly, flat nosed, paunchy, bolt-eyed little man stood in the court convicted of offending the government. When the court asked him to seek pardon for his offences and to be free of his charges, he said "If you propose to acquit me on condition that I abandon my search for truth, I will say, I thank you O Athenians, but I will obey God, who as I believe, set me this task, rather than you and so long as I have breath and strength I will never cease from my occupation with philosophy. I will continue the practice of ushering in whomever I meet and saying to him, are you not ashamed of setting your heart on wealth and honours while you have no care for wisdom and truth and making your soul better? I know not what death is - it may be a good thing, and I am not afraid of it. But I do know that it is a bad thing to desert one's post and I prefer what may be good to what I know to be bad."

He drank the hemlock and embraced death, but never parted away from truth. He overcame the biggest hurdle that any man can ever dare to face - death! He was Socrates.

Socrates was an unimpressive and repulsive looking man. But he was one of the greatest philosophers the world ever produced. He enjoyed the reputation of being the world's wisest man. He always remained shabbily dressed and wandered all over Athens since early morning. His mission was to spread true knowledge to all in country.

He was confronted with two main charges. The first was that he refused to obey the Gods of the Republic and second that he tried to pollute the minds of the youth of Athens. Socrates refuted both the charges vehemently saying that he believed in the one and only universal God and that it was his solemn duty to acquaint the people with Truth. It was his desire to make his fellow citizens happy and to uphold the command of the God.

Socrates did not yield before pressures and continued his crusade against the untruth. He became the founder of Moral Philosophy and almost became responsible for bringing the 'heavens down to the earth'. He never bothered himself with abstract metaphysics rather laid emphasis on the truth concerning life.

Socrates, after his death, ultimately occupied a special place in the hearts of every philosopher, thinker and intellectual - not only by his quality of skills or reason but by his capacity to win every hurdle even at the cost of his life and maintaining confidence in his concepts and ideas. This clearly exhibits the greatness of the soul that he possessed.

Winning Over Odd Circumstances

Man usually becomes a slave of his circumstances. Whenever he faces hardships or agony, he reels under its effect and develops a tendency to give up. If his circumstances make him weep, he weeps, if his circumstances make him laugh, he laughs. Hence, he becomes a slave of time and destiny. A man who wants to dash ahead towards a great life has to learn the art of winning over circumstances.

Circumstances always have an impact upon the mind and not on the individual. People fall victim to circumstances because they lack control over their mind. If a girl has a nasty row with her mother, she would not even enjoy watching her favourite movie on the television. In a nutshell, if a person knows how to control his mind, he can actually win over any circumstances.

Expect Nothing From Others

You will only be bound by circumstances if you begin to expect anything from anybody other than yourself. Sorrow or dejection is only bred if your expectations remain unfulfilled. Hence, try to be as self-dependent as possible.

Do Not Worry About Results

If you work with a good motive, you will definitely get the desired results. If not, then do not brood over results. It is the hope of results that binds you and never the action that you commit.

Believe in Yourself

Whatever your circumstances are, never lose faith in yourself. If you lose wealth, you have lost nothing, if you lose health, you can still regain it, if you have lost your family, you can still survive in this world but if you lose faith in yourself, you are as good as dead. Even God helps those who help themselves. Listen to your conscience and proceed further with your plans. The world has given such iron-men who have weathered every storm as a tribute to their mission.

Within a span of 60 years, a man who experienced the entire gamut of human experiences ranging from poverty to riches, failure to success, amiability to enmity and humility to unquestioned power was an ordinary man. He was none other than Mohammad.

Mohammad was born in 570 AD - a time when Mecca was implicit with the grossest superstitions and idolatry. At the tender age of 6, when Mohammad was barely beginning to understand the world, he lost both his parents and was left alone in the world. His Uncle Abu Talib, who soon developed a deep affection for the child, brought up Mohammad. At the age of twelve, Mohammad set out for a long journey to Syria along with his uncle, where for the first time he came across people from different faiths, races and beliefs.

Most of his youth was spent in tending sheep and goats in Mecca. The most remarkable feature of his personality was that whatever duties came to him, he completed them with utmost precision and sincerity, whether it was grazing animals or remembering the Lord.

Deeply religious by nature, Mohammad would often retire to the silent caves at the foot of mount Hira for plunging into prayers and deep meditation. It was then that he had several spiritual experiences and revelations. He took a pledge to spread the message of God to all of the humanity.

Amidst the bitterest oppositions, banished, stoned, humiliated and his very life at peril, Mohammad fearlessly continued to proclaim his new message of spirituality.

Today, at the commencer
more than 450 million arde·
He triggered off one of the
man had ever witnessed
rock against all opposit·
lished Islam.

Trust God

To achieve a great mission, on~
strength. This strength can only co~
Trust in God acts like a shield against ev~
stance. Feel the living and moving presence
moment of life. This will help you to maintain y~
rium in difficult times. Take adversity to be the gih
for drawing you closer to Him. Make your life a silent pra,
Make your work worship, eat as an offering to Him, ana
sleep as a peaceful obeisance to Him, talk as a divine chant
in praise of Him. Try to meditate on His divine picture - it
will give you immense strength and peace of mind. When all
doors are closed, His doors are always open.

Here is the story of a young lady who faced every difficulty to accomplish her noble task towards humanity.

Florence Nightingale

"The Lady with the Lamp" has become a great and legendary figure in the history of Britain. She was a lady who sacrificed all comforts and personal happiness for pioneering clean and devoted attention to the sick. It was during the Crimean War that Nightingale lit a lamp that continued to give light to those who were suffering in pain and illness in the lap of disease and death. Modern nursing and hospital owe to Florence Nightingale a lot.

It was 1850 which saw a terrible revolt and bloodshed in war. A young woman endowed with all good things of life, well bred, properly educated and yet obsessed with a flam-

...ve humanity and follow the path of serving ...against her family and social customs to de-...to nursing the poor. Within five years of her ... revolt against rigid social norms, she emerged ... figure, loved by all and cherished by the rich and ...alike. That woman was none other than Florence ...gale.

...rence Nightingale was born at Florence, in Italy in ... on May 12. Her parents were affluent and well-con-...ed. They were associated with leaders in politics and ...iety. They were repugnant to the fact that their younger ...aughter was thinking to take up a career that would bring her in touch with the fearful conditions in hospital life. They used every possible method to impede her from following that path. She was thrown open to parties, outings, sojourns as well as comforts but nothing could stop her.

Wherever she went across Europe, she always looked for places where some noble task was being undertaken for the needy and the afflicted. After her Continental travels, she was determined to take up a career that she thought would make her life worthwhile. She was soon to realize, that during those days women were encumbered from following the path of service to mankind owing to social prejudices.

The only question she asked to herself was **How could I overcome all that?**

It was during those days that Florence Nightingale met a man who made a lasting impression on her mind. His name was Sydney Herbert. Florence developed a strong platonic bond with Herbert because of humanitarian impulses that were common to both. She was tall, elegant, slender and serene but she preferred to use her qualities in humanitarian work rather than in settling down for a comfortable married life.

Through the cogent intervention of Sydney Herbert, her family gradually yielded before her wishes. She enrolled

herself at Fleidner's Pioneer
proper establishment for h
strict austere life and unde
up during dawn, did al'
with other sisters and
To a person who was
it was a life of complete
actually it was an experience
that at last she was achieving the
essary for the noble task to which
dedicate her life.

Thereafter began her noble career in the fie
The Crimean War broke out in September 1854. On
21, 1854, she set out with a group of nurses and cre
history. She almost became an immediate celebrity. Here
was a gentlewoman, affluent, sophisticated, young and
attractive who was prepared to renounce a life of luxury to
face dangers, trepidation and uncanny toil. But she had to
confront with one of the biggest problems - circumstances.
There broke a severe prejudice against her by the sectarians.
She was denounced for the very organization of her relief
party. A woman taking charge of a man's job! People were
simply not ready to bear with this fact. But Florence
Nightingale paid no heed to the critics. She continued her
tirade against suffering.

She was laughed at when she began to cater to the
wounded soldiers. She began to provide books, amusements
and cafes for the injured. Before Florence took up
this yeoman's task, the condition of hospitals was deplorable.
The nursing profession was absolutely disreputable
and nurses used to be selected from the unwanted sections
of the society. Nurses used to be vulgar, drunken, unhygienic
and immoral. Yet, this was the profession to which Florence
Nightingale gave her heart and soul believing it to be
the best vocation for a woman as an offering to the Lord.
She overcame defamation, physical suffering as well as

...in order to provide honour to the profession... ...r daily routine, that late at night or in the early ...e morning, when all her staff would retire, she ...erself to make a last trip around her wards with a ...amp in her hand. She came to be known as the lady ...e lamp and continues to inspire the present genera-... ...ith her flaming compassion.

She never allowed difficult circumstances to overtake ...er. Rather she had the undying courage to trample upon all difficult circumstances. Deep within herself she had the conviction that what she was doing was right - in her own eyes as well as in the eyes of the Lord. She remained confident about her mission.

Before her death she got the answer to the question which she often asked to herself - What is to become of me? She had the greatest satisfaction to realize that her mission had been accomplished.

It was Lord Stanley who said, "I know no person besides Miss Nightingale who, within the past hundred years within this island, or perhaps in Europe, has voluntarily encountered dangers so imminent, and undertaken offices so repulsive, working for a large and worthy object, in a pure spirit of duty towards God and compassion for man."

The Foes of Greatness

The question that may confront you now is, which are the impediments or foes of Greatness? They are:

Wastage

The first foe of greatness is wastage, wastage can be of anything. It can be of talent, time, resources or energy. People who keep their talents concealed due to some fear, weakness or scarcity, actually commit a crime on themselves. Talents are a gift given by God for the welfare of mankind. Those who hide their talents commit an offence against the the Lord. Keep it in mind. NEVER WASTE YOUR TALENTS. If you are good in sports try to play for your country, if you are a good artist, produce some beautiful pieces of art. If you are a writer, write for the betterment of mankind. People, who while away their time in gossiping, watching movies and wandering aimlessly waste their valuable time that can otherwise be used for significant pursuits. People who achieve greatness, realize the value of time. Again there are some, who waste their physical and mental energies in evil pursuits. Indulgence of any sort saps out the vital energy of any person. Therefore, one must always try to avoid physical indulgences.

Procrastination

"A stitch in time saves nine" is a very old saying which implies that a work done on time saves unnecessary botheration and leads to success. Some people have the habit of delaying a work without any substantial cause. As a result of this, a lot of their plans are either shelved, or kept pending till the last moment. This is one of the biggest weaknesses which most of the people have. If procrastination can be controlled, the success of a person will be a lot more convincing.

Inconsistency

Some people have the habit of starting a work with too much of zest but leaving it mid-way without completing it. This reduces confidence and credibility of a man. Any task undertaken must be accomplished till the end. For this, it is very important to break a big task into small parts and concentrate upon those parts one by one till success is ensured in each one of them. An inconsistent person can rarely achieve success in any field.

Lack of Confidence (Timidity)

Timidity reduces the charm of a man's personality. A timid

person finds it difficult to take bold decisions, to communicate to an audience as well as in putting his viewpoint across others. Many a dream has been shattered because of timidity. The only way to overcome timidity is to face every obstacle headlong. Even if you confront failures, consider them to be a part of your struggles. Failures always add charm to a work. A work achieved with utmost difficulty has great value. Hence shed off timidity.

Monotony

When a person falls short of new ideas and feels hesitant to work upon novel areas of activity, he falls a victim to monotony. Monotony is significantly instrumental in reducing the productivity of a particular task. Whatever work is done without ample interest fails to generate positive results. On the other hand, anything that is done innovatively is bound to yield prolific results. We can see this in the life of inventors and discoverers who played with new ideas and gave to the world marvellous discoveries. One such person was William Caxton.

William Caxton

Not because of the skill he founded, nor for the pragmatic accomplishment of his enterprise, is the fame of William Caxton immortal in the world of printing. It was because of his mission to remove ignorance and spread knowledge as the pioneer of the Printing Press that his name still remains alive even after more than five centuries of his demise. Pioneers become immortal not because of their practical achievements but because of their strength to conceive something new and put it before the world. They continue with their journey in untested waters without bothering about the results of their pursuits.

William Caxton was born around 1422 in Kent, England. About the age of 14, he worked as an apprentice with a mercer named Robert Large for a period of three years. When he was just 19, Robert Large expired leaving about 20 Marks in his will for Caxton. After the death of Robert Large, William joined another company where he was responsible for solving the disputes between different merchants, supervising the import and export of goods and safeguarding the commercial interest of England. William Caxton was extremely pious and industrious. He always remained enthusiastic in whatever task he undertook. But his life was destined to change for he was burning with the desire to spread knowledge. His mission was to perpetuate books having the highest moral and literary value. The path that he clearly chose was to illumine the lives of his countrymen by circulating hundreds of copies of best literature at very reasonable prices since in those days hardly a dozen copies were available for those who were quite rich. Written matter was very expensive. The letters were not very readable and the presentation used to be shabby. William Caxton changed all that. He established his small printing press. His journey towards greatness and self-confidence began when in 1478, he printed the first edition of Chaucer's **Canterbury Tales**. Soon after that books began to flow out from Caxton's tiny press.

Caxton's zeal was astonishing. He slogged day in and day out in editing, translating and setting. He loved publishing those books which he believed were suitable for public benefit. He began his stint with spiritual works in order to elevate the spirit of morality in society.

William Caxton's pioneering efforts began to attract other players in this field. Oxford, Lettou and Lithuanian were soon to follow. But none could undermine the contributions of William Caxton.

Caxton always gave more significance to the essence than on the appearance. Devoutness, ethics and intellectual worth were always the requisites for choosing the books. He never refused the works that could expound erudition among his countrymen. Caxton printed all those ideals by which he survived. He was not only England's first Printer but also one of her first educators, a trend-setter and an establisher of scholarly trends.

It can be said about William Caxton that he left the world in harness with a silent prayer flowing from his pen for the betterment of mankind. He was not only a pioneer of a mechanical invention called the 'Printing Press' but also of a unique concept of elevating mankind with the light of mass education.

The Greatest Comebacks in Human History

After bathing in the chilled waters of the bay of Fundy one hot day, a young man was crippled because of infantile paralysis. From the waist downwards, his body became totally numb and motionless. His career seemed to have ended. All his dreams seemed to have come to a naught. But this man refused to accept defeat. Inspite of the negative remarks given by the doctors, he was determined to make a comeback - and he actually did. It was no mean comeback for a man who had become totally handicapped. In 1932, when U.S.A. was still in the grip of financial slump and mass unemployment, he startled the world by becoming the President of the United States of America and guided her through the most trying times in the World History.

Franklin D. Roosevelt was a man of firm convictions. He was a vigorous reformer and an eminently practical man. His various schemes of Rehabilitation as well as his iron will and self-confidence steered the nation successfully through the Second World War.

His success as a person as well as a President proved the fact that - even the gravest of storms can be crossed, if the person has the will to do.

No great life has remained free from obstacles. These men have fallen a thousand times from their missions yet they were capable of maintaining the spirit of their work. The history of the world has innumerable instances where people have made the most startling comebacks and regained their power, wealth and position. A living example before the readers has been the life of **Nelson Mandela** who became the first President of South Africa and freed his nation from slavery even after spending about three decades in prison.

A person is capable of making a comeback from any phase of his life. He only needs to keep the fire glowing within him. Failures are a testing ground for assessing the internal strength of a person. What make persons' astounding comeback are:
- *The blessings of his parents*
- *Unflinching devotion towards God and*
- *Faith in himself*

In the worst of times, a person must undertake as much good deeds as possible. Because what he requires most is not wealth or support, but blessings. Blessings from others can produce miracles in life of a person because it comes out from the deepest core of a person's heart. Seek blessings of God, of your parents, teachers and also of those who are poor, downtrodden and miserable. It works as a divine power.

During periods of extreme stress, the golden rules to be followed are:

1. Regular Prayers

You must pray twice a day for fifteen minutes daily. It develops your confidence as well as helps you to face adversities boldly. Regarding the significance of prayers, Mahatma Gandhi used to say that as food is required to sustain the body and thoughts are required to sustain the mind, similarly prayer is required to sustain the soul and enhance its power. That is the only time when you are with yourself, isolated from the bickerings of the and free to restore your mental peace. Prayer is a ...ary requisite for every person aspiring to become great. Along with prayer the reading of Scriptures like the **Bhagwat Gita,** the **Bible** or the **Koran** will give great peace of mind and supreme Self-confidence.

2. Silence in Speech

During adverse circumstances, try to remain choosy with words. This will help you to conserve your energy. Retire to a solitary room and contemplate upon the possible solutions. Think but do not worry. You will think better in silence when the mind is pacified. This will help you to avoid foul language, excitement and mental stress. This was the main reason why people in Ancient India preferred to spend most of their times in mountain caves and forests where they could remain alone and work upon their inner strengths.

3. Equanimity in Feelings

Whether the times are good or bad, they never remain the same. Hence, try to maintain your emotional equilibrium all the time. If happiness comes, believe it to be the grace of god and if sorrow comes, take it to be a test to gauge your power. Those who begin to crumble beneath adversity are not fit to undertake a mission in life.

4. Realizing the Temporariness of Conditions

You must always realize the fact that time and conditions never remain constant. They are like the moon, waning and waxing all the time. Hence, if good times did not stay with you for a very long time, then bad times would also not continue. Feel the ephemeral nature of time and develop a sublime peace within yourself.

Lord Krishna in the **Bhagvat Gita** says, "He who remains same in heat and cold, pleasure and pain, happiness and sorrow, him I call a Yogi." This is actually the true definition of greatness.

Greatness does not require any large platform, rather it requires great virtues.

The Great Virtues

Greatness is not based upon big deeds. A person can become truly great in his everyday life with the help of small deeds.

The saints and sages in our country have ascertained certain virtues, which have the power of ascertaining the greatness of any person. These great Virtues are:

Kindness

Kindness must not be restricted towards Human Beings only. It must also be exhibited towards animals and lesser humans as well who cannot preserve themselves. For this reason only in Hinduism, there is no greater sin than animal slaughter.

Forgiveness

One who has learnt the lesson of forgiveness, has truly learnt the essence of forgiveness. It is indeed very difficult to forgive a person who has wronged you. But instead of keeping ill feeling and burning with the fire of vengeance, one must learn how to forgive. This will give you immense satisfaction. It is the easiest way of winning people and making them walk on the right path.

However, there are certain deeds that are unpardonable. What are they?

Non-Violence

The second and probably the greatest virtue is that of Non-Violence. When almost the whole world is burning in the fire of hatred and vengeance, what is required most are soldiers of Peace who can bring harmony in today's conflict ridden society. A man who is non-violent is contributing a lot more to society than that person who although committed to good deeds adopts violent means to fulfil his ends. The path towards greatness can only be reached with the vehicle of Peace & "Ahimsa". There have been many tyrants and despots in the world who succeeded in becoming 'big' in the eyes of the world but miserably failed to achieve even a spec of greatness. Non-violence does not mean resisting evil. Some people who are physically and mentally weak claim to be non-violent. But cowardice should not be mistaken as non-violence. A non-violent man is he who is strong enough to cause harm but does not possess the desire to do so. On the other hand, a coward is he who burns with vengeance but lacks the strength to avenge, hence turns non-violent. Hence non-violence should come out of kindness and forgiveness and not out of fear or cowardice.

Humility

Another great virtue that is worth mentioning is that of humility. Some people have the habit of taking credit of whatever good they have done. They believe in blowing their own trumpets. Whatsoever noble a deed may be, if the doer talks about his own glories and accomplishments, the deed certainly loses its sublimity and renders it futile. If you do good to someone, never talk about it. A sacrifice that you make must never be extolled by you. Our scriptures regard it as one of the greatest sin. Thank the recipient, for he is giving you an opportunity to do something noble and worthwhile. Humility is certainly a precious ornament of great men and women.

Tolerance

Today, most of the problems in the world are due to intolerance. There is intolerance with relation to caste, creed, religion and sex. Intolerance is infact a limitation of thoughts. In some cases it arises because of jealousy. If a person begins to put himself in the shoes of another, he can definitely overcome intolerance. The root cause of this folly is a false sense of pride, or an insecurity from the other's viewpoint. Those who have become great in this world have embraced every single thought that has benefitted mankind instead of confining themselves in water-tight compartments of rigid opinions. An intolerant person can only arouse hatred because of his narrowness. Hence Swami Vivekananda had rightly commented "Expansion is life, contraction is death."

You can begin your journey towards greatness now with the help of the ideas presented by me in this humble work.

Success Through POSITIVE THINKING

—*S.P. Sharma*

Is half full better or half empty?
* *Choose right* • *Think better*
* *Live well*

Present-day life has become too complex and complicated. There is a scramble for more and more. Money, power and wealth have become symbols of success and happiness. A confused sense of affairs and lopsided values that's leading to a lot of tension and distress.

Now **Success Through Positive Thinking** shows you the way out. Advocating a change of attitude through moderation, acceptance of things as they are, and inculcating of moral values. The result? A positive personality free of negative elements like anxiety, stress, greed, envy and jealousy!

An Overview

Success Through Positive Thinking shows you the right path to real happiness through:
❖ A proper perspective on life
❖ Meditations and prayer
❖ Importance of work
❖ Handling of criticism and slander
❖ Knowing the difference between right and wrong, real and unreal
❖ Proper channelizing of sexual and physical energy.

Demy size • Pages: 178
Price: Rs. 80/- • Postage: Rs. 15/-

Skills for Excellence

— *Luis S.R. Vas*

How do you achieve excellence in a world of growing complexity and rapid technological change? The first step is a thirst for excellence. This is the motivation to achieve quality in whatever you do. Around the world numerous consultants have combined insights from behavioural sciences to train people in achieving excellence in various realms. But excellence requires skills in various areas.

In **Skills for Excellence** the author has brought together within one volume most of the ideas and practices which are being taught in enterprises around the world. The book starts with achievement motivation and shows how, as research has proved, this skill can be cultivated and developed. The other skills presented in this book are innovativeness drawn from the ideas of Peter Drucker and others; thinking skills from the concepts developed by Edward de Bono; a problem solving technique devised by Rudolf Flesch; creativity as taught by Robert Fritz.

There is also time management, learning ability, communication skills and your retention powers. An equally basic but often neglected skill is the ability to maintain your health and fitness. All these skills are covered at length adapting ideas from masters in their respective fields.

Demy size, Pages: 176
Price: Rs. 88/- • Postage: Rs. 10/-

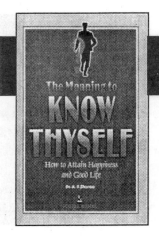

The Meaning to KNOW THYSELF

By: **Dr. A.P. Sharma**

How to Attain Happiness and Good Life

Envy, jealousy, hatred, anger, fear, greed, selfishness, the negative feelings and emotions tend to poison our personalities and lead to tension and unhappiness.

The only way to check these feelings and enhance the positive aspects is through self-knowledge. One sure way to achieve inner harmony and happiness.

Now **"The Meaning to Know Thyself"** helps you attain it through the wisdom of the greatest and most revered minds and books. With the essence of Pluto, Aristotle, Buddha, Jiddu Krishnamurti and others all distilled and presented in most readable lucid style. Offering the most practical approach to decipher the unvirtuous thoughts, dispel anger, fear and selfishness and in turn achieve a pure self and attain inner harmony and happiness:

The Book Includes
+ Buddhists' masters and monks lively discussions
+ Comparative views of Eastern and Western philosophers
+ Similes and myths from great masters.

Demy size, Pages: 128
Price: Rs. 60/- • Postage: Rs. 10/-

The Complete Guide to
MEMORY MASTERY

—*Harry Lorayne*

**ORGANISING & DEVELOPING
THE POWER OF YOUR MIND**

The memory is always present; ready and anxious to help if only we would ask it to do so more often.   —Roger Broille

The more intelligible a thing is, the more easily it is retained in the memory, and contrariwise, the less intelligible it is, the more easily we forget it.   —Benedict Spinoza

Thinking is the hardest work there is, which is the probable reason why so few engage in it.   —Henry Ford

Don't thou love life! Then do not squander time, for that is the stuff life is made of.   —Benjamin Franklin

Here, in one volume, you will learn his unique proven techniques to:

- Increase your powers of memory and concentration.
- Strengthen good habits and discard bad ones.
- Improve your powers of observation.
- Deliver a speech without fear.
- Become more organised and time-efficient.

**Big Size • Pages: 312
Price: Rs. 160/- • Postage: Rs. 20/-**

How to Develop A Super Power Memory

—*Harry Lorayne*

Tips to develop amazing memory capabilities

"From the world's leading expert on mind and memory training, here is the most practical, lucid and definitive memory-training book ever written." — *MoneyLines Magazine*

This is one of the all-time classics from the all-time best-selling author of memory-related books. Make your brain work for you. Scientists say we use only 10% of its capacity. Get the edge. Tap into your most precious resource and unleash the natural powers within you. You will never again have to be told anything twice...

TV infomercial star Harry Lorayne reveals his positive methods of developing a photographic memory. If knowledge is powerful then memory is super powerful!

You will increase your memory capacity by tenfold and learn to accurately recall anything, anytime, anywhere - such as:

- Prices • Phone Numbers • Names • Codes • Details • Facts
- Orders • Book Passages • Jokes • Directions • Instructions
- Conversations • Dance Steps • Dates/Places • Game Strategies
- Battle Plans • School Work • Lectures • Speeches

Big size • Pages: 168
Price: Rs. 120/- • Postage: Rs. 20/-

Banish Fears and Negativity
The Secret of Letting Go

—Guy Finley

Whether you need to let go of a painful heartache, a destructive habit, a frightening worry or a nagging discontent, *Banish Fears and Negativity* shows you how to call on your own hidden powers and how they can take you through and beyond any challenge or problem. This book reveals the secret source of a brand-new kind of inner strength.

In the light of your new and higher self-understanding, emotional difficulties such as loneliness, fear, anxiety and frustration fade into nothingness as you happily discover they never really existed in the first place.

With a foreword by Desi Arnaz Jr., and introduction by Dr. Jesse Freeland, *Banish Fears and Negativity* is a pleasing balance of questions and answers, illustrative examples, truth tales, and stimulating dialogues that allow the reader to share in the exciting discoveries that lead up to lasting self-liberation.

This is a book for the discriminating, intelligent, and sensitive reader who is looking for *real* answers.

Demy Size • Pages: 240
Price: Rs. 96/- • Postage: Rs. 15/-
